# CONCILIUM

THEOLOGY IN THE AGE OF RENEWAL

# CONCILIUM

# CONCILIUM/VOL. 50

SCRIPTURE

# THE
# PRESENCE
# OF GOD

edited by PIERRE BENOIT, O.P.
ROLAND MURPHY, O. CARM.
BASTIAAN VAN IERSEL, S.M.M.

## VOLUME 50

*CONCILIUM*
*theology in the age of renewal*

PAULIST PRESS
NEW YORK, N.Y./PARAMUS, N.J.

PAULIST PRESS
EXECUTIVE OFFICES: 304 W. 58th Street, New York, N.Y. and 404 Sette
   Drive, Paramus, N.J.
*Publisher:* John A. Carr, C.S.P.


EDITORIAL OFFICES: 304 W. 58th Street, New York, N.Y.
*Executive Editor:* Kevin A. Lynch, C.S.P.
*Managing Editor:* Urban P. Intondi


Printed and bound in the United States of America by
Wickersham Printing Co., Lancaster, Pa.

# CONTENTS

## PART II

### BIBLIOGRAPHICAL SURVEY

## PART III

### DOCUMENTATION CONCILIUM
Office of the Executive Secretary
*Nijmegen, Netherlands*

# PREFACE

Pierre Benoit, O.P./*Jerusalem, Israel*
Roland Murphy, O.Carm./*Washington, D.C.*
Bastiaan van Iersel, S.M.M./*Nijmegen, Netherlands*

M any people today are troubled by what has been called "the death of God", but the thought haunts them for different reasons. Some would be glad to be rid at last of a superstitious belief which they feel may have been spontaneous in an age of ignorance, but which has become futile in our age of science and technology. Others, however, fear to lose contact with that higher being who, they feel, must necessarily be there, with whom they want to converse and whom they would like to love, but who keeps silent and hides himself. And so the absence of God has become a source of relief for some, a source of distress for others, and an enigma for all.

This problem is not new. The mystery of a God who is both present and absent, who imposes himself on us, yet eludes us, has worried man in every phase of his history. The people of the Bible also had to face this problem. One might even say that their whole religious adventure can be summed up as a tormenting search for a God who offers himself to them, yet never allows them to grasp him. It is the everlasting struggle of Jacob with the angel, the attempt to seize the unseizable: "I will not let you go unless you bless me. . . . Tell me your name" (Gen. 32, 27. 30). To the God of the Bible this harsh combat is a means of testing the growth of his people. He hides himself so that he

1

may be found. For man it was a long journey during which, guided and fortified by God, he discovered, little by little, the ways of faith, obedience and love which led him to the true encounter with God in Jesus Christ.

The problems of the people of the Bible were not the same as ours, and their solutions do not immediately apply to us. Nevertheless, the fundamental anxiety is the same, and the means to overcome it, taught by God himself, have a perennial value. That is why even today man turns again to those sacred pages where he rediscovers his own difficulty and where he can listen to those constantly repeated summonses which alone can help him to get out of his impasse. And this is what the present volume of *Concilium* invites him to do.

The first two articles outline the divine dialectic of presence and absence in the course of biblical history (de Vaux) and in the revelation of the Word (McCarthy). That God guides his people, chastises them and delivers them is the conviction of all, the basic belief in the saving God of Exodus. And yet, how many moments of darkness and apparent incoherence occur! Why did the chosen people and so many of the just have to pass through those adversities? His ways indeed are not ours (cf. Is. 55, 8). It is true that he speaks to privileged individuals, the prophets, who convey his message to the people, but how much is obscure, even there! Do we ever know whether it is really God speaking? And are the most definite pronouncements not also the most baffling?

To understand this situation, the man of the Bible examines himself. Why does this alienation exist between creature and Creator? He finds a first answer (Schreiner) in his conscience: he realizes that he is a sinner who has fled from God by rebelling against him. If he wants to return to him whom he has discarded from his life, and who has driven him from paradise, he will have to repent and patiently wait for God's mercy and forgiveness which alone can restore him to the lost presence of God. And God, in his goodness, promises him that forgiveness. But this is not the end of the matter. Even just men like Job feel that God is far away. Man then receives a second answer (Larcher) from the Spirit, who teaches him that God is beyond man by the whole extent of his transcendence. No one can see God, and not die as a result (cf. Ex. 33, 20). There is an abyss between the finite and the infinite, and this abyss can only be bridged if the Most High deigns to make himself accessible and finally to raise man to his level. That, too, God promises. The Bible is full of announcements and gestures that pave the way for this encounter. He will come! He is coming! Both God and his messengers use all kinds of images to express this: Word, Spirit, Wisdom, Messiah, Servant, Son of Man—all expressions that contain the promise of his presence.

All these promises and gestures lead to Jesus Christ. He bridges the twofold abyss which separated man from God by his person and his labor. As Savior he washes away the iniquities of the sinner and helps the prodigal son to return to the Father. As the Word made flesh, he brings the presence of God near and makes it possible for us to approach him: "Philip, he who sees me sees the Father" (Jn. 14, 9).

Later, in a volume devoted specifically to christology, we shall study all that is implied in the incarnation insofar as Christ's being and conscience are concerned. In this volume we limit ourselves to two specific aspects of this encounter between God and man in Jesus Christ: on the one hand, the presence of the Father's love as expressed in the power of Jesus' works (Crossan); on the other, the way in which Christ manifests the image of the creating and re-creating God, who restores in those who are saved the image of adoptive sons which they lost through sin (Luz). Henceforth the presence of God is again restored to any man who repents and surrenders himself in a faith of trust. In such a man God dwells through the Spirit of his Son (Lyonnet). Through this faith and its sacraments, man meets God with his whole being, body and soul. In this life the faith is still in darkness and man still feels the pain of God's absence, but he is also certain of a presence that is very close. Finally, through the Christian—through all Christians who constitute the Church—the presence of God is offered to the world, to all creation, through the message of the Good News and the sacralization of all temporal and material values (Murphy-O'Connor).

These are the answers man finds in the Bible to help him in his anguish created by the absence of God. And these answers remain valid (Worden). Scientific pride, intoxicating technology, an anthropocentrism which causes man to become blind when confronting his own presence—all these modern forms of idolatry are but the new aspects of an everlasting problem. Without being intimidated by the phenomenal progress in the world's evolution, but, on the contrary, seizing hold of it and making it serve a better life, the Christian can and must find and establish there the presence of God in Jesus Christ. God is only absent in appearance; he is very close in reality to anyone who seeks him with humility, faith and love. This presence of God which becomes real through man's union with Christ finds expression in two powerful phrases of St. Paul: "Christ in us" and "we in Christ", which are studied in the Bibliographical Survey.

# PART I
## ARTICLES

Roland de Vaux, O.P./*Jerusalem, Israel*

# The Presence and Absence of God in History According to the Old Testament

Man, as we see him in the Bible, was convinced that God was present and active in his own history and in that of his people. But his experience also told him that God could remain hidden in history or withdraw from it altogether. In this article we shall examine these two distinct experiences.

## I

### THE PRESENCE OF GOD IN HISTORY

#### God's Intervention in History

God intervened first of all in the history of individual people. He called Abraham and told him to leave Mesopotamia and to betake himself to Canaan (Gen. 12, 1-5). He was "with" Jacob when he was staying with Laban (Gen. 28, 30; cf. Gen. 31, 5. 42), telling him to return to Canaan (Gen. 31, 3) and later to go to Egypt (Gen. 46, 3). In Canaan as in Egypt God would be "with him". God called Moses (Ex. 3), whose life would from then on be motivated by divine commands until God stopped him by his death on the threshold of the promised land (Dt. 32, 49-50; 34, 4). At the time of the Judges it was Yahweh who

7

roused the liberators of Israel (Jgs. 3, 9. 15; 6, 14), when the Spirit of Yahweh came upon them (Jgs. 3, 10; 6, 34; 11, 29; 14, 6. 19; 15, 14). It was God who chose Saul to be the first king of Israel (1 Sam. 9, 16; 10, 17-26), God's chosen one (Ps. 78, 70; 89, 4). If Solomon succeeded David in spite of court intrigues, it was because Yahweh had so decided (1 Kgs. 2, 15). It was a prophet who brought Jeroboam to the throne in the name of Yahweh (1 Kgs. 11, 29f.), and another prophet who told Basha that he had been made king by Yahweh (1 Kgs. 16, 6), and still another who anointed Jehu in the name of Yahweh (2 Kgs. 9, 3). The prophets themselves were called by God. God spoke to Samuel (1 Sam. 3), took Amos away from his flock (Am. 7, 15), appeared to Isaiah and Ezekiel in his terrifying majesty (Is. 6; Ezek. 1), forced Jeremiah to take up his vocation (Jer. 1, 4-10), and brought a reluctant Jonah back to his duty.

God also intervened in the history of Israel as a whole. When he called individuals, it was to invest them with a mission to the people. The prophets were God's messengers. The king was the vassal of Yahweh, who himself was the true king of Israel (1 Sam. 12, 12; cf. 1 Sam. 8, 7). Moses was the leader who had to take the people out of Egypt, impart the law to them in the Sinai desert and guide them to the borders of Canaan. All these prophets were God's heralds or instruments, but it was God who acted. At the deliverance from Egypt it was he who "threw horse and rider into the sea" (Ex. 15, 21); it was he who provided the people not only with water in the desert (Ex. 15, 25; 17, 1-8; Num. 20, 1-11), but also with manna and quail (Ex. 16; Num. 11). "Yahweh is a warrior" (Ex. 15, 3), the "God of the armies" (1 Sam. 17, 45). There existed a "Book of the Wars of Yahweh" (Num. 21, 14) which is now lost, but up to the time of David the wars of Israel were thought of as started, waged and won by Yahweh. This is the way in which the Old Testament speaks of the conquest of Canaan under Joshua, the wars led by the Judges, and the wars with the Philistines; Israel is "a victorious people in Yahweh" (Dt. 33, 29). With the establishment of the monarchy, war became desacralized, but victory was still ascribed to Yahweh (2 Sam. 8, 6. 14; 1 Kgs. 20, 13. 28; 22, 6. 12; 2 Kgs. 3, 18). When Sennacherib had already occupied the fortified towns of Judah, Isaiah announced that Yahweh would save Jerusalem (Is. 37, 33-35).

Jerusalem was indeed the "City of Yahweh" (Is. 60, 14), the place chosen by Yahweh as a home for his name (Dt. 12, 11; 14, 25, etc.). The God of Sinai came down from his mountain (Dt. 33, 2; Jgs. 5, 4; Hab. 3, 3) and from one encampment to another trekked along with his people (2 Sam. 8, 7), the ark being the symbol of his invisible presence (Num. 10, 34-35). With the ark he made his entry into the temple that Solomon built for him and lived there in the darkness (1 Kgs. 8, 10-12).

But these divine interventions in history are not all beneficial because this Savior is also Judge. He "visits" Sarah and Anna and grants each a son (Gen. 21, 1; 1 Sam. 2, 21); he "visits" the people in order to set them free (Gen. 50, 24; Ex. 4, 31), but he also "visits" the sinful and the rebellious to punish them and vindicate himself (Am. 3, 2. 14; also cf. frequent examples in the prophets). It was Yahweh who rejected Saul (1 Sam. 15, 26), destroyed the houses of Jeroboam (1 Kgs. 14, 10), Basha (1 Kgs. 16, 4) and Achab (2 Kgs. 9, 7-9), and decreed the fall of the kingdom of Israel (2 Kgs. 17, 22-23) and finally that of Judah (2 Kgs. 23, 27; 24, 20).

But God is also seen to intervene in the history of other peoples in the Old Testament. The God who made Israel leave Egypt also made the Philistines come from Caphtor and the Syrians from Kir (Am. 9, 7). Egypt was his people and Assyria was the work of his hands (Is. 19, 25). He called Cyrus by his name, making him his anointed one and his instrument (Is. 41, 25; 44, 28; 45, 1-3). But at the same time he chastised Damascus, Philistia, Phoenicia, Edom, Ammon and Moab for their crimes (Am. 1, 3—2, 3), "visited" the king of Babylon as he had visited the king of Assyria (Jer. 50, 18), and destroyed the cities, kingdoms and empires from Egypt and Babylon to distant Elam (Jer. 46—51).

## God's Direction in History

Those interventions are not mere accidents in the historical development of individuals and nations. God directs history as such. His deeds are announced before they take place. His threats are followed by the actual chastisement, and his promises hold until they are fulfilled.[1] Abraham is promised a son (Gen. 15, 4; 17, 19-21; 18, 10), and Sarah gives birth to Isaac (Gen. 21, 1-2). As history develops, there is an expansion of promise and fulfillment. Abraham's descendants were to be slaves in Egypt but God would deliver them from the situation (Gen. 15, 13-14). God came down to Egypt with the sons of Jacob, but ensured their return (Gen. 46, 4), and so the covenant with Abraham led to the deliverance under Moses. But this was only one phase. Yahweh set his people free to bring them to a land flowing with milk and honey (Ex. 3, 8), and he drove out the inhabitants (Gen. 34, 11) because it was the land promised to the fathers (Gen. 12, 7). In Solomon's days, after the last Canaanite enclaves had been wiped out and David had created a kingdom, the Yahwist chronicler wrote the history of his people from the call of Abraham to the conquest as a continuous and rich fulfillment of promises.[2]

But the bright days of David and Solomon were followed by a series of dark moments. David's "empire" disintegrated, the kingdom broke up, victory passed to the Aramaeans, Assyria first annexed a part of the kingdom of Israel and then laid hold of Samaria, deporting its inhabitants, the kingdom of Judah was laid waste by Sennacherib, and finally the Babylonians devastated Jerusalem, sending the greater part of the people into captivity. Those, too, were seen as the deeds of Yahweh. His promises stood, but the sins of the people and their leaders provoked his

[1] For the theme of "promise and fulfillment", see especially W. Zimmerli, "Verheissung und Erfüllung," in *Evangelische Theologie* 12 (1952/3), pp. 34-59.

[2] For this and what follows, see also M. Burrows, "Ancient Israel," in *The Idea of History in the Ancient Near East,* ed. R. Dentah (1955), pp. 99-131.

intervention as Judge. In the prophets, the theme of threat and chastisement runs side by side with that of promise and fufillment Toward the end of that period, the author of Deuteronomy developed a theology of history as a series of ups and downs in his narrative of the events from the conquest to the exile, from the book of Joshua to the end of the books of Kings.[3] It is set out at the beginning of the book of Judges (Jgs. 2, 11-19): periods of oppression and peace, of setbacks and successes, alternate according to whether the people continue to sin or repent. The argument is pursued throughout the history of the monarchy. It is spelled out in detail in the observations on the fall of the kingdom of Israel (2 Kgs. 17). Yet God's promises remain valid and persist in David's descendants. The great Deuteronomist history ends with the favor bestowed on Jehoiachin, symbol of the end of the captivity and the dawn of salvation (2 Kgs. 25, 27-30). Second Isaiah announced the end of the exile. Yahweh, who had summoned Babylon to bring down Jerusalem, would now deliver Babylon into the hands of Cyrus who was chosen to liberate the captive Israelites (Is. 44, 28). There would be a new exodus, a reentry into the promised land, more marvelous than that in the days of the ancients (Is. 43, 14-21; 49, 8-12; 52, 7-12). Cyrus signed the decree allowing them to return to Jerusalem "to fulfill the word of Yahweh that was spoken through Jeremiah" (Ezra 1, 1; cf. Jer. 25, 12).

This belief in God's active presence in history might lead to an underrating or denial of man's part in the affairs of this world, a kind of quietism. This tendency in fact can be seen in certain texts. In the narrative of the exodus from Egypt, when God's intervention was decisive for the whole history of the people, Moses said: "Yahweh will do the fighting for you; you have only to keep still" (Ex. 14, 14). The Chronicler rewrote this history in the same vein—for instance, when he relates the war against Ammon, Moab and Edom (2 Chr. 20, with a reference to Ex. 14, 14): "You will not need to fight there. Take up your

[3] This expression is taken from G. Goossens, "La philosophie de l'histoire dans l'Ancien Orient," in *Sacra Pagina* I (1959), pp. 242-52.

position, stand firm, and see what salvation Yahweh has in store for you" (2 Chr. 20, 17). Many other texts, however, particularly old ones, stress the human contribution along with divine assistance. This double causality [4] appears in the Song of Deborah (Jgs. 5) and in the recital of Gideon's campaigns (Jgs. 7). The great story of the succession to the throne of David (2 Sam. 9—20 and 1 Kgs. 1—2) only mentions human actors, but it is prefaced by Nathan's prophecy (2 Sam. 7, 5-16), where God promised the throne to the descendants of David, and it concludes with Adonijah saying that the crown eluded him and fell to his brother Solomon, "since it came to him from Yahweh" (1 Kgs. 2, 15).

## Parallel Texts from the Ancient East

Other peoples of the Ancient East also believed that their gods intervened in history, and non-biblical texts provide striking examples of this belief.[5] Mesha, king of Moab, attributes his successes and setbacks with neighboring Israel to his god Kemosh: "Kemosh . . . has saved me from all the other kings and made me triumph over my enemies. As to Omri, king of Israel, he humiliated Moab for a long time, because Kemosh was angry with his country. . . . Kemosh said to me: 'Go and take Nebo from Israel.' . . . The king of Israel had fortified Yahaz and resided there when he fought against me, but Kemosh drove him away. . . . Kemosh said to me: 'Go down, and fight Hauronen,' and I went down . . . and Kemosh has dwelt there from my days on." [6]

Yahweh delivered Canaan and its inhabitants into the hands of the Israelites (Jos. 2, 24). In the same way Tushratta, king of Mitanni, says: "When the enemy penetrated into my land, Teshub,

[4] I. Seeligman, "Menschliche Heldentum und göttliche Hilfe. Die doppelte Kausalität im alttestamentlichen Geschichtsdenken," in *Theol. Zeitschr.* 19 (1963), pp. 385-411.

[5] B. Albrektson, *History and the Gods. An Essay on the Idea of Historical Events as Divine Manifestations in the Ancient Near East and in Israel* (1967).

[6] J. Pritchard (ed.), *Ancient Near Eastern Texts Relating to the Old Testament (ANET, ²1955)*, p. 320.

my Lord, delivered them up to me and I vanquished them." [7]
Nebuchadnezzar uses the same language: "I have subjected to
Babylon the numerous peoples whom Marduk, my Lord, delivered up to me." [8] The kings of Assyria went to war on
the command of their god and, on their return, they rendered
an account of their victories because he fought with them. For
all their pride they recognized the double causality—human and
divine—of history. In one place Salmanasar III breaks off the
recital of his campaigns to say: "At this moment I paid homage
to the majesty of the great gods and exalted the heroic exploits
of Assur and Shamask for posterity by erecting a stele repre-
senting myself as king, and I have written on it my heroic conduct and my deeds in battle." [9] Assarhaddon relates how he
broke the revolt of his brothers: "The terrifying glory of the
great gods, my Lords, crushed them, and they lost their senses
when they saw the attack of my powerful front line. Ishtar, the
Lady of the battle, who loves me and made me her high priest,
stood by my side, snapped their bows and dispersed their battle
lines." [10]

When there was a severe famine, David consulted Yahweh
and learned that this was the punishment for the breaking of the
oath by Saul that he had sworn to the Gabaonites. David
pacified God by granting the Gabaonites the reparation they
demanded (2 Sam. 21, 1-14). Under Mursil II a plague devastated the Hittite kingdom. Mursil consulted the oracles and
was told that an oath sworn by his father had been broken and
that this had provoked the wrath of the god of thunder. Mursil
confessed his father's fault and so tried to appease that god.[11]

The gods are considered to direct history according to a plan
that they work out but which they can modify. Sennacherib had
destroyed Babylon and razed the temple of Marduk to the ground.

[7] J. Kundtzon, *Die El-Amarna Tafeln* (1907), n. 17, pp. 32-34.
[8] S. Langdon, *Die neubabylonischen Königsinschriften* III (1912), pp.
18-20.
[9] *ANET*, p. 277.
[10] *ANET*, p. 395.
[11] *ANET*, p. 289.

But his successor Assarhaddon explained that this was a punishment inflicted by Marduk himself upon the citizens of Babylon for their sins. The god had fixed a term of seventy years for this punishment. Marduk, however, was merciful—his wrath lasted but a moment—and he ordered them to begin the restoration of the city in the eleventh year.[12] This text reminds one not only of "Yahweh slow to anger" (Ex. 34, 6; Num. 14, 8) and the seventy years of Jeremiah (Jer. 25, 11; 29, 10), but above all of the interpretation given in the Bible of the fall of Jerusalem and the return from capivity as acts of God's justice and mercy.

## Specific Features of the Religion of Israel

In spite of what the biblical and non-biblical Ancient East have in common, the Old Testament notion of God's presence in history shows features that are specific to the religion of Israel. This is true, first of all, in its doctrine about God. In regard to the universe he has created and governs, Yahweh is the one God whose sovereignty cannot be shared with any other. This uncompromising monotheism results in one single history in space and time. It becomes the history of God's relations with the world from its origin until its consummation. Yahweh is also infinitely closer to his human beings than are the pagan gods to their followers. As Deuteronomy expresses this thought: "And what great nation is there that has its gods so near as Yahweh our God is to us whenever we call to him?" (Dt. 4, 7).

There is above all the special relationship between this living God and Israel.[13] He had chosen Israel from among all other people to be his own people. This election and this covenant became the central point of Israel's faith. Yahweh is the God of Israel and Israel is his people. But this relationship did not originate outside time, in a mythical past. It was the result of God's intervention in history, the deliverance from Egypt, and this event gives meaning to the whole of history, before and after.

[12] D. Luckenbill, *Ancient Records of Assyria and Babylonia* II (1927), par. 642-43.
[13] H. Gese, "Geschichtliches Denken im Alten Orient und im Alten Testament," in *Zeitschr. f. Theol. u. Kirche* 55 (1958), pp. 127-45.

It had been prepared by the call of Abraham and the promises made to the fathers. It was not an end but a beginning. The covenant was not a fact limited to the past, but a continuous reality which from then on dominated the whole of history. In all other regions of the Ancient East the plans laid by the gods cover but a short chain of events.

Because Israel is Yahweh's people, it owes obedience to its God. If the people are faithful they will be blessed; if they are rebellious, there will be punishment. I have already pointed out that this "up-and-down" interpretation of history was also current among other Oriental peoples, but because the election persists and the covenant can be restored after man has failed, inasmuch as God's gifts are irrevocable, good shall ultimately prevail, and this up-and-down movement of history tends toward an end, even if this end will only be achieved at the end of man's days. This belief in God's presence in history, constantly confronted with the hard reality of history itself, is the very root of hope for the future and of eschatology. Therefore, together with the concepts of monotheism and of the election and covenant, messianism is also an exclusive feature of the religion of Israel.

## God's Presence in History and the Faith of Israel

These interventions by God in man's history are the basis of the faith of Israel. And among these, there is first of all the great saving deed of Israel's deliverance from Egypt. The narrative of this event ends with these words: "Israel witnessed the great act that Yahweh had performed against the Egyptians, and the people venerated Yahweh; they put their faith in Yahweh and in Moses, his servant" (Ex. 14, 31). The statement that "Yahweh made Israel leave Egypt" is the briefest and most frequent confession of faith. We find it in every period, from the oldest parts of the Pentateuch to the last books of the Old Testament, in every literary form and in the most diverse circumstances.

Even the more developed confessions of faith are essentially summaries of history. Every year, at the feast of the first fruits, every Israelite had to recite: "My father was a wandering

Aramaean. He went down into Egypt to find refuge there, few in number; but there he became a nation, great, mighty, and strong. The Egyptians ill-treated us; they gave us no peace and inflicted harsh slavery on us. But we called on Yahweh, the God of our fathers. Yahweh heard our voice and saw our misery, our toil and our oppression; and Yahweh brought us out of Egypt with mighty hand and outstretched arm, with great terror, and with signs and wonders. He brought us here and gave us this land, a land where milk and honey flow" (Dt. 26, 5-9; cf. Dt. 6, 20-24). Another example is the conclusion of the covenant at Shechem, which is preceded by a reminder of all that God has done for his people (Jos. 24, 2-3).

This belief in God's presence in history is also expressed in the liturgy. The feasts of Israel commemorate the saving deeds of Yahweh. The celebration of the Passover, an old spring festival of nomadic times, coincided with the flight from Egypt. After the Israelites had settled in Canaan, they celebrated the Passover and the feast of Unleavened Bread in springtime, when both feasts reminded them of their deliverance (Ex. 23, 15; 34, 18; Dt. 16, 1. 3. 6; cf. esp. Ex. 12, 24-27). Later on the feast of Tabernacles (tents) served to commemorate their sojourn in the desert (Lev. 23, 43), while the feast of Weeks (Pentecost) became the commemoration of the covenant of Sinai, perhaps already mentioned in 2 Chronicles 15, 10.

God's interventions in the Israelites' history had great value for their faith and the way it was expressed in their worship, and as a result the recital of the events assumed transhistorical dimensions. At the time of the deliverance from Egypt an event took place which the modern historian cannot trace in detail, but which he is forced to admit because such an event is necessary to explain the faith and the very existence of Israel, even as a people. It was a deliverance in which the group of people, led by Moses, saw the hand of their God. When that memory, together with the belief in Yahweh, had become the common possession of "all Israel", the event became the inaugural act of the national epos and its miraculous character was emphasized (Ex. 14); it gave rise to the triumphal poem of Exodus 15, the high-soaring lyricism of Psalms 78, 105 and 135, and the long paraphrase of Wisdom 10, 15—11, 21 and 16—19. On the other hand, the linking of this memory with the feast of Passover turned the deliverance from Egypt into a liturgical celebration (Ex. 12—13). In the same way, the modern historian surmises that the settlement in Canaan was a slow and varied process in which different groups proceeded separately. But this occupation of the Holy Land was the fulfillment of the promises. National tradition welded these actions together, and the book of Joshua presents the process as a rapid conquest achieved by the cooperative efforts of the twelve tribes, led by Joshua with the miraculous assistance of God. This is the way in which faith expressed a history directed by God.

## II
### THE ABSENCE OF GOD IN HISTORY

### God's Self-Concealment in History

The development of this sacred history is a process in which light and darkness alternate: God conceals himself there as much as he shows himself. Along with the recognition of God's interventions, whether saving or punishing, the Israelites often asked throughout their history: "Where is God? What is he doing?" Then they would answer this question themselves in different ways, from the grumbling of the people in the desert to the skepticism of Koheleth. The Israelites complained to Moses that he had only brought them out of Egypt to let them perish (Ex. 14, 11), and that he had led them into the desert to die of hunger and thirst (Ex. 16, 3; 17, 3). God gave them manna but they grew tired of it and asked for meat (Num. 11, 4-6). God sent them quail, but they gorged themselves and died of overeating (Num. 11, 31-34). They understood nothing. Later, when they were oppressed by the Midianites, Gideon asked the angel of Yahweh: "Forgive me, sir, but if Yahweh is with us, then why is it that all this is happening to us now? And where are all the wonders our ancestors tell us of when they say, 'Did not Yahweh bring us out of Egypt?' But now Yahweh has deserted us" (Jgs. 6, 13). The basic article of faith is thus recalled and doubted.

This complaint of Gideon is echoed in Psalm 44, which mentions the victories won by God's "right hand" and God's "arm" as "our ancestors have told us", and then turns to the misfortunes and humiliation that beset the people, finally crying out: "Wake up, Lord! Why are you asleep? Awake! . . . . Rise! Come to our help!" (Ps. 44, 24-27; cf. Pss. 77, 10-11; 35, 22-23; 59, 5). "Yahweh, why do you stand aside? Why do you hide from us now that the times are hard?" (Ps. 10, 1). This same distress is found in the prophets. At moments of calamity Jeremiah asks: "Is Yahweh no longer in Zion? Is her king no longer there?" (Jer. 8, 19). During the captivity Israel laments: "My destiny is hidden from Yahweh" (Is. 40, 27), and Zion complains: "Yahweh has abandoned me; the Lord has forgotten me" (Is. 49, 14).

The answer given by the psalmists and the prophets is that these absences of God are only illusory; they are meant to serve as a punishment for sins, to exhort to repentance and to pave the way for new saving deeds. God hides himself so that people will return to him and look for him. But this always brought with it the temptation to look for other "presences", those of the Canaanite gods, who were supposed to distribute the goods of this earth. Even before going into the Promised Land the people committed apostasy to the Baal of Peor (Num. 25), and later on Hosea had to remind them that it was Yahweh who gave them their corn, their wine and their fresh oil (Hos. 2, 7. 10). They were also tempted to rely on other sources of help. The kings forgot that they were only the vassals of Yahweh, and believed that they directed the course of history. They put their trust in their chariots and horses, seeking the alliance of Assyria or Egypt (Hos. 5, 11; 7, 13; 12, 2; Is. 30, 1-7; 31, 1-3) when there was no other Savior than Yahweh (Hos. 13, 4; Is. 43, 11).

## God's Apparent Withdrawal from History

It even happens that God seems to withdraw from history altogether and allows it to proceed counter to his plan. Josiah had won full independence for Judah from Assyria and had reconquered a large part of the Assyrian provinces between which Israel had been distributed. At the same time he had brought about a radical religious reform, suppressed pagan practices, restored the temple, established the center of worship in Jerusalem, applied the regulations found in the rediscovered book of Deuteronomy and renewed the covenant with Yahweh. After this reform, and in the midst of this new national prosperity, the first redaction of the Deuteronomist history was brought to an end on a note of unrestrained praise for Josiah: "No king before him had turned to Yahweh as he did, with all his heart, all his soul and all his strength, in perfect loyalty to the law of Moses" (2 Kgs. 23, 25). His success was seen as the reward for his loyalty and the vindication of that theology of history, delineated in Deuteronomy 6, 1-3, which the Deuteronomist historian had applied to all the kings of Israel and Judah. More than any other, this model king had drawn the blessing of God on himself and his people. But in 609, as a result of his efforts to oppose the plans of Pharaoh Neco to come to the rescue of Assyria, Josiah was killed at Megiddo, and Judah fell under Egyptian overlordship. From the point of view of faith this was a profound shock. The fact is reported with intentional brevity in the continuation of the Deuteronomist history (2 Kgs. 23, 29), and no word was said about this death which could not be explained if God really directed history.[14]

Thirty years later Jerusalem was conquered by Nebuchadnezzar, the temple destroyed and the inhabitants deported. This was a still more grievous test of Israel's faith, for actual history seemed to be proving false the religious interpretation of history, the repeated promises of salvation, the enduring character

[14] S. Frost, "The Death of Josiah. A Conspiracy of Silence," in *Journal of Biblical Literature* 87 (1968), pp. 369-82.

of Israel's election and the covenant, and the belief in the inviolability of Jerusalem, the city of Yahweh, and of the temple, the house of Yahweh. One might conclude that Yahweh had failed in his promises and abandoned his people. The short book of Lamentations made a painful contrast between the devastated city and the glorious image the people kept of Jerusalem, "the loveliest of all, the joy of the whole world" (Lam. 2, 15; cf. Ps. 48, 3). However, it also gave the theological solution: [15] this devastation is still an act of God, who punishes the unfaithful city but does not reject it forever and ever (Lam. 3, 31-33). And the book ends with a prayer and a vow (Lam. 5, 21-22).

The "history of salvation", the *Heilsgeschichte,* so often mentioned today, is retrospective. God's plan in history and the meaning of that plan only become clear when the plan itself is fulfilled. The Old Testament basically presents us with a "history of judgment", an *Unheilsgeschichte,* and the continuity of God's plan of salvation is only shown in the fulfillment of the promises—i.e., in the salvation brought by Jesus Christ. Those who walked the crooked path of history walked in faith and in hope. Living ourselves in the new phase of history, opened up by the resurrection, we have to proceed as our fathers did in the Old Testament, strengthened by the certain knowledge that God continues to direct history, and cooperating with him in working toward the final establishment of his kingdom.

[15] N. Gottwald, *Studies in the Book of Lamentations* (1954), pp. 47-62; B. Albrektson, *Studies in the Text and Theology of the Book of Lamentations* (1963), pp. 214-39.

Dennis McCarthy, S.J./*St. Louis, Missouri*

# God's Presence and the Prophetic Word

I n Exodus 12, 12 it is God himself who destroys the Egyptians
and saves Israel. In an even older
tradition about the same event, as found in Exodus 12, 23, is a
mysterious being, the destroyer, who acts as the agent or power
of Yahweh to accomplish the same ends. Without doubt the
destroyer is a remnant of very primitive beliefs in malevolent
powers which menaced the young lambs. In Wisdom 18, 14-16
we read of the same event: "While soft silence enveloped all
things, and the night was half gone in its swift course, your
all-powerful Word leaped from heaven, from the royal throne
. . . a stern warrior carrying the sharp sword of your command,
and stood and filled all things with death. . . ." In this very latest
of Old Testament books, the Word has supplanted the primitive
destroyer and made it unnecesary for God himself to come to do
the task as in Exodus 12, 12. Nor was the Word of God merely
destructive. Surely the best known record of the power of that
Word is the magnificent picture in Genesis 1, 1-2. 4a, where the
simple divine *fiat* causes the whole mighty panorama of creation
to unfold. This too, though older than the Wisdom text, is
relatively late in the form it has in our Bibles. Thus we can see
some pattern of development: belief that God's power and
presence were to be found in his Word, and not only in himself
or in personified agents.

The idea of the powerful Word is, in fact, very old. In the third millennium B.C. the priests of Memphis told of the creative power of the word (literally, "tongue") of their god Ptah. Probably this ancient Oriental concept (by no means confined to the Memphite theology) was not entirely unknown in Israel. However, we must ask how belief in the presence of God and God's power in the Word grew in Israel, for in view of the development so briefly outlined in the first paragraph it is clear that this belief was not universal and normative from the beginning. In large part the answer to this question comes readily enough. It was through the prophets that the presence of God in his Word became manifest. Hosea, one of the first of the prophets to give his name to a book of the Bible, was directed to give his children symbolic names, for to the ancients the name was somehow the thing itself and portended its being and destiny. This appears very clearly when the change in what one was called meant a change in reality: ". . . instead of what was said of them, 'Not my people,' it shall be said of them, '[They are] sons of the living God' " (Hos. 1, 10). Thus without a doubt God was present in his Word, for that Word could give life itself. The obvious problem, when it is a question of the prophetic Word, is the difficulty of recognition. The Word was and is not easy to grasp. God is present in his Word, but where is his Word present? That is the agonizing question, for "God spoke in many and various ways", and the very richness of this gift makes it no easy task to discern the true Word of God. When Yahweh proclaims through his prophet that "my thoughts are not your thoughts, nor your ways my ways" (Is. 55, 8), he is not merely separating his ways from those of wicked men, as Isaiah 55, 7 might seem to imply. He is asserting that what is of God is so totally different from anything else that merely human means may be insufficient to understand what he says and thus what he is.

This is all too easily documented. Men naturally misunderstood the promises characteristic of certain psalms and repeated in some of the words of Isaiah (Is. 29, 1-8; 37, 35) that Zion, its temple, and its city of Jerusalem would be inviolable. They took this as some kind of magic formula guaranteeing of itself the presence of God and his protection, as though the presence depended on the words and not on what they might be. This is what Jeremiah found (Jer. 7, 1-15), and though he denounced it, men continued to act in ways incompatible with the divine presence. The result was that the presence deserted its chosen place, though not the prophet, for it is Ezekiel (cf. Ezek. 8—11) who sees and announces not exactly the utter disappearance of God but, as it were, his displacement. Often, if men did not more or less deliberately misunderstand the prophet, they turned from him and followed designs which were not those announced in the prophetic Word, as indicated in Isaiah 8, 11-15 and so often in the life of Jeremiah. The result might be ruin, or it might well be silence in which God hides himself from his people (Is. 8, 16).

The Word of God, then, is not easy to recognize so that one can find God in it and follow him. There was no simple external sign to guarantee that *this* was God's Word. In the relatively unsophisticated days of Saul, a condition approaching frenzy might be accepted as a sign of a true prophet (cf. 1 Sam. 10, 9-13; 19, 18-24), but this could so obviously be misleading that it soon fell into discredit. Nor was the holding of authentic office from God enough. In the great passage giving Nathan's promise (2 Sam. 7, 1-17) we have the king, the one anointed by the choice of Yahweh himself; he was to be especially close to him, his son (Ps. 2, 7) and agent on earth, whose protection of justice—that is, right order—guaranteed the right order of nature —that is, rain and crops in due season (Ps. 72; cf. 2 Sam. 23, 3-4). Moreover, the very "spirit of Yahweh" could speak in him; the Word of Yahweh was on his tongue (2 Sam. 23, 2). Thus the king had prophetic powers—and not just any king in this case, but the special favorite of Yahweh: David.

In 2 Samuel 7 this man, the authentic leader of God's people and endowed with prophetic traits, surveys his situation. He has achieved a united state for the people of God, put down their enemies, and brought the ark of the covenant to his capital, Jerusalem. To him it seems unfitting that he, a mere man, should dwell in a palace of sorts while the ark, the special, visible sign of the divine presence in Israel, remains in a simple tent. He decides to provide something better for it. Surely this is fitting and reasonable. Moreover, the king consults Nathan, a true prophet, who immediately agrees with David, "for Yahweh is with you", as he says. Surely this decision represents the Word, the wish of God as far as any man can reasonably be expected to know. Yet it is not. The very night after the decision had been made, the Word of Yahweh did in fact come to Nathan, and it flatly contradicted all that had been said. David is not to build a temple ("house") for God; God will rather build a dynasty ("house"—the kernel of the original term of Yahweh plays on the double meaning of the Hebrew word "house") for David!

The whole sequence as it now stands in 2 Samuel 7, 1-17 is undoubtedly more complicated than this. It has grown under the impetus of the desire to explain why David himself did not build a temple, to show that David's dynasty had not been rejected like Saul's, and to integrate David into the overall Deuteronomistic view of history, among other things, and this has been done by accumulating additions to the prophetic Word. However, the heart of the story is old, and, old or new, its lesson is clear. Man's best thoughts, an office from God, even possession of the Spirit—none of these assures us that we have God's Word. Hence the terrible uncertainty of the divine presence in the Word.

That the dilemma is literally terrible is shown in the teaching of 1 Kings 13. A man of God—this is an older designation of a prophet—has an authentic and detailed mission to Jeroboam at Bethel. He carries it out faithfully up to the point where an old prophet intervenes. This other prophet is surely sincere, for the words "he lied to him" at the end of verse 18 seem to be a gloss, grammatically irregular in the Hebrew text and hardly in keeping with verses 20ff. Nevertheless, he turns the man of God aside from the directions he originally received from "the Word of Yahweh". The result is destruction for the man of God. He had not been entirely faithful to the Word given to him. One is reminded of Galatians 1, 8: "Even if we or an angel . . . preach a gospel contrary to that which you have received, let him be accursed." It would surely be difficult to stand up for the Word received in the face of an apostle or an angel. The man of God in 1 Kings found it impossible to resist a recognized prophet, abandoned the Word, and died for it. No doubt this story has grown in the telling, but this only emphasizes all the more that the stakes are high indeed, for God's Word cannot fail of its ultimate purpose, but a man can fail to recognize or receive it to his cost.

This applies not only to the men who meet God through the Word mediated by a prophet but also to the prophet himself. It was always true that the Word of God made great demands on him. A common Hebrew word for prophecy means simply "burden", and it probably had connotations beyond those of a concept such as: "The burden of the message was. . . ." It hints that the call to proclaim God's Word imposed hardships on a man, giving him an uncomfortable role with duties he might not want and deprivations at which he would normally rebel. It is easy to create for ourselves a false image of the prophet as a person full of self-assurance and secure in his possession of the Word. In fact he gave up much, and he faced the same problem as others. He, too, had to discern where the true Word of God was. And if he were to mistake the Word of God as did the man of God who spoke to Jeroboam, might he not face a similar fate? It was a matter of essential importance for him to be certain that the Word which presented itself to him was truly from the Spirit of God. Yet the Old Testament never supplies entirely satisfactory criteria for determining this (nor does anything else, for that matter). To be sure, a true prophet tended to foresee hard things (Jer. 28, 5-9), not to speak on the strength of dreams (Jer. 23, 25-28), to be disinterested (Mic. 3, 5), and to be orthodox (Dt. 13, 1-5). But none of these norms by themselves, nor taken all together, are absolute. They might help to determine the truth of something, but they could not assure that it was the true, prophetic Word of God. The criterion of the fulfillment of a prophecy (Dt. 18, 22) is a little better, perhaps, but it is usually of no immediate use, and in any case the fulfillment of the prophetic Word is often unexpected and obscure.

In view of all this, it is easy to understand the reluctance of someone like Jeremiah to assume the prophetic office (Jer. 1, 6-7). Even the feeling of assurance that one had the true Word of God did not offer an easy life; rather, the contrary was true. When the Word demands a total dedication, forbidding even a family (Jer. 16, 2), it is no wonder that the prophet could be rebellious and in need of consolation (Jer. 15, 19-21; 20, 7-12). Even Ezekiel, to all appearances a far more rugged individual than Jeremiah, needed encouragement: "Listen to what I say; be not rebellious" (Ezek. 2, 8). Inasmuch as Ezekiel was called on to do and to say things which have led men to question his mental balance even to the present day, we should not be surprised at this need. We all want to appear impressive to our neighbors and to history.

Prophet, king, and commoner, then, all faced the same problem of discovering the Word in which God might truly be found, even though they realized that the demands of that Word could be great. The wonder is not that the prophet himself sometimes felt and usually met doubt and rebellion. The wonder is rather that the Word was listened to by anyone at all. Despite this, however, there was some listening, as the result of stern pedagogy. In part this pedagogy is to be seen in the very hard sayings themselves. They call upon man to accept God and his Word on God's terms, and not merely on human ones. That is, by drawing man from himself they point to God in his Word, but they do not make the process of acceptance easy. The desired goal is for man to recognize God in his Word, but the mere fact that he does is no guarantee of happiness or success. Amos heard the Word, and he had to leave his simple life and his home to preach in a foreign kingdom before a hostile audience (Am. 7, 10-14). Considering his message, the hostility is hardly surprising. He called for justice from those who profited from injustice. He placed Israel on a parallel with its despised enemies (Am. 1, 3—2, 3. 6-11). He went so far as to point out that its privileged position called for extra penalties for failure (Am. 3, 2). His demands are absolute; there is no compromise: obey and it may be possible to escape doom (Am. 5, 14-15). No wonder that a tradition developed that the true prophet would have hard things to say!

Isaiah contributed to this tradition. He believed in his nation, and he may have been close to court circles. At least he had ready enough access to the king. Yet he took up Amos' theme of justice and reinforced it. The justice of the chosen people must be like that of its God, whose justice is his holiness (Is 5, 18), which made it an absolute beyond anything imaginable by a creature. This call to be just and holy as God is just and holy may be noble, but it is a terrible burden to put on men. Then there was Isaiah's insistent demand to put trust in Yahweh and not in armies and alliances—once again, an absolute. This is no call for saying "in God we trust" while maintaining a reasonable defense establishment and a shrewd network of treaties. It is a call to lean on God alone (Is. 7, 1-13; 28, 14-15. 30-31). King and people were not ready for this, of course; they were not prepared to see God in this Word (Is. 6, 9-10) any more than they had been ready to listen to Amos and Hosea a few years earlier in the kingdom of Israel, the northern and larger of the Hebrew kingdoms into which David's empire was split after the time of Solomon.

The simple fact is that the people of God failed to see God in the prophetic Word. It is hard, and they rejected it and him. The results varied in detail, but they took two general directions. The more obvious is the fact that the disasters foreseen by the prophet occurred. Amos spoke to the people of Israel, but they would not "seek Yahweh and live" (Am. 5, 6). They continued as before, and soon there was the destruction and exile so vividly pictured in most of Amos' oracles. Judah, too, paid a price for turning to human help rather than the prophetic Word. Jerusalem was not taken, but all the countryside was laid waste by the erstwhile Assyrian ally. This violent pedagogy fits the theory of schooling at the time, whose basis definitely was the maxim: "Spare the rod and spoil the child," and the men of that era might have seen this kind of history as the rod writ large. Nevertheless, it was destined to continue, with the seeming failure of Amos and Isaiah repeated in Jeremiah and beyond.

However, we should also look at the other direction taken in the divine pedagogy, as seen in the prophets—namely, the use of silence, which is something very different from, but often as eloquent as, the Word. Yahweh hid his face from a rebellious people (Is. 8, 17), which in that context meant that he would not speak through the prophet for a while. The sovereignty of the Word of God is clear. No man commands it, not even a prophet. We also find silence as explicit pedagogy in Ezekiel (Ezek. 3, 24-27), but as is so often the case, it is most poignant in Jeremiah. Unwillingly the prophet had been seized by forces leading a meaningless, hopeless rebellion against the Babylonians who had conquered and destroyed Judah. Some direction was urgently needed, but even though the prophet prayed, God remained silent for ten agonizing days. Only after this delay did the Word come to Jeremiah (Jer. 42, 10). Ironically, although the fact was consistent with all of his experience, the Word was immediately defied by the very ones who had sought it. In fact, the vignette in Jeremiah 42—43 is a summary history of the prophetic Word. The whole sequence of events took place amid the general ruin of Judah which had followed upon the failure to heed the prophet. The Word was there, but given by God and not commanded even by the prophet. Men hear it but do not obey, and tragedy results—here for Jeremiah himself, who is carried off to Egypt against his will.

In most of what has been said we have distinguished prophet and people. Of course we have seen that the prophet, too, had the problem of recognizing the true Word of God. But even beyond that we should not make the distinction too sharp. The prophet belonged to the people. He suffered with them. If this is best expressed in Jeremiah's cry: "Is there no balm in Gilead? Is there no physician there? Why then had the health of my people not been restored? O that . . . my eyes were a fountain . . . that I might weep day and night for the slain . . ." (Jer. 8, 22—9, 1), it is implicit in the tenderness of a Hosea, and the love of Isaiah for Jerusalem surely took in its countryside which he saw ravaged. Ezekiel, emphasizing the prophetic action as a means of communication parallel with the Word, symbolically joined the suffering of the final siege of Jerusalem (Ezek. 4, 1-8) and the following exile (Ezek. 12, 1-7), even though he was already in Babylonia as part of the earlier deportation (2 Kgs. 24, 15-16). Perhaps the prophet himself did not need the insistent pedagogy of ruin after disobedience, but he shared it. Neither did he need the lesson of silence as others did, unless we conjecture that this was part of the penalty and penance of Jeremiah already discussed. Rather, it must have been part of his regular, though unrecorded, experience when we reflect on the relative paucity of words he received compared with the long periods of activity of Hosea, Isaiah, Jeremiah and Ezekiel.

And what is the lesson to be learned from all this? The prophetic Word, so hard to recognize, was often frustrated, and all suffered. Instead of the Word there was frequently only silence. This made for an uneasy history at best, but still a fruitful one, for it made it possible to see something of the ways of God. His Word must be heard one way or another, for it is always sovereignly effective. But it takes much time to learn to listen. Merely threatening the consequences of not listening was not enough; those consequences had to be experienced. However, things could not stop at this, for it seems to leave us with a picture of a God characterized by his vindictive justice.

There is far more than this to be learned. God will indeed have justice from and for everyone, but this is a positive step from mere vindication. However, it simply puts him in the category of many another divinity—for example, the sun god who was widely believed to be, and often appealed to as, a guardian of justice in the ancient Near East. Yahweh will have more, a perfect faith in himself, utter trust which seems to fly in the face of sound political reason (as in Isaiah 7, 9), or at least in the face of overwhelming pressures (as in the whole career of Jeremiah). Probably such faith, which could later on at least be confirmed by the rightness of the hard sayings of the prophets, was and is the only means by which the justice demanded might be gained. After all, possessions give a great feeling of security, and it is difficult to see men giving them up, even though they had been acquired by shady means, much less abandoning the means themselves, in the prosperous years of Jeroboam II during which Amos and Hosea spoke. These two must have sounded like religious cranks, rebels who were trying to unsettle an established order that was quite satisfactory, at least to those who counted. And then there were Isaiah and Micah condemning injustice, idolatry, and alliances which showed a lack of total trust of God. For their pains they saw their country ruined and their capital impoverished. How much saner things must have seemed under the reign of Manasseh, when men compromised and enjoyed some peace and prosperity! There was still much to be learned.

But there is another kind of security even more inimical to the total trust in God demanded by the prophetic Word. This is the security of being sure of one's own rightness. After all, the men of Judah had before them the lesson of what had happened to their northern brethren. Seeing their land stripped by the invader when the king failed to follow the lead of Isaiah was part of their history, too. But that condition was righted by making a small compromise under a succeeding king. Apparently, when we compare Isaiah 29 with Jeremiah 7, the only lesson learned was that the temple was a talisman securing the capital city, no matter what they were in themselves. They did not need a prophet to bring God into their midst; he was present and protective in his temple. The people had to be deprived of this illusion that they had easy access to the presence of God if they were to acquire a trust in God alone and be righteous as God wanted—hence the value of the lesson of exile. If they wished to learn from it, they would be able to seek the Word of God successfully and God in his Word. Lest the lesson be lost, a favorite theme of Ezekiel was that their earlier failures and their present hardness of heart had closed them to this Word, even though they claimed to seek it (cf., e.g., Ezek. 14, 3. 10; 20, 3).

All this is reasonable and true as far as it goes, but there is more. If the divine pedagogy of the prophetic Word working itself out in history taught so much, it also revealed the only possible source of the required justice and faith. Ultimately it can only come from God: "Behold, I am laying in Zion . . . a precious cornerstone", a basis of faith and justice (Is. 22, 16-17). For God is just, but he is also loving, and his love includes—or, in the strong imagery of the prophet, overpowers—his mere will to justice: "I will not execute my fierce anger, I will not destroy Ephraim; for I am God and not man, the Holy One in your midst. . . ." (Hos. 11, 9). So stated one of the earliest of the classic prophets. He is echoed by one of the latest, Deutero-Isaiah during the period of the exile, when he assures us that Yahweh will have mercy because his Word is always effective, and it promises an eternal covenant (Is. 55, 6-13). However, these are the words of a prophet who can and does reflect the story of the prophetic Word which took place during the two hundred or so years between him and Hosea. For two centuries men had expected salvation from God, a salvation more or less in accord with their own ideas, which usually meant (and means) possessions, protection and victory. There had been the prophets to protest against this, to say that God was to be found not in these things but in trust and justice, but they had not been listened to. Now, after all these years and all this confirmation of the prophetic message, the remnant of Israel could understand that indeed God's ways are not man's, and God's ideas are not man's. They must accept salvation on his terms, which means righteousness based on trust in God's overwhelming love.

The lesson would seem to have been clear enough, and it had been driven home with overwhelming emphasis. Nevertheless, it had to be repeated, and in explicit terms. We learn this from some post-exilic texts. After the return it was necessary for another prophet to point out that God had indeed spoken through the prophets, but he had been disregarded, and it was this which had brought upon the people the horrors of the conquest and exile (Zech. 7, 8-14). It is true that these verses are the prelude to a hopeful picture of the new situation, but the very need to say them, and to say them so explicitly, hints that all is not as it should be in Jerusalem, a point which the history of the time shows to have indeed been the case. But really, it is superfluous to corroborate a prophet from history in this way, for one thing about the prophetic Word is its immediacy. In it God is present now, and while a prophet may draw on history for some reason or another, it is always with a view to bringing God to his hearers now, not to recalling the past for its own sake. Still, in the post-exilic period, Malachi is even more clear. With all their concern about worship—no mean thing in itself—verses such as Malachi 3, 1-10 sound like the earliest prophets in their insistence on justice and their emphasis on judgment.

It is worth our while to note passages like these last two, if for no other reason than the universal tendency to treat the later prophets as epigones who have nothing to offer. On the contrary, they carry on the message, admittedly with different emphases and less verbal skill. We should expect the change of emphasis, for, as we have said, the prophetic Word was meant to bring God's presence to the prophet's own time, and one would hardly be a prophet if he ignored the concerns of his own audience, different though they may have been from those of earlier or later generations. There is a real value in all this. On the one hand, it brings out the divine will to have his Word heard and thus made present to his people. If their situation demanded a new emphasis, new areas of interest, the Word could accommodate itself to these so that it could be heard. It could also accommodate itself to lesser linguistic skills.

This teaches us a little more about how God is to be met in his Word. To demand that the Word conform to the taste or interests of any epoch, as though that were the normative time (and this is a great temptation, for every age thinks of itself as the mature one and would measure everything by its own concerns) is once more to demand that God and his Word conform to man's ways and man's ideas. This also holds true for the quality of expression. The Word need not be great poetry, any more than it need promise security or success or conform to a particular epoch's concept of what is important. In fact, whenever we seek these things in the Word or expect them from it according to our own understanding of them, we seek to judge the Word on our terms. God is not to be found in that way. If the prophetic Word has anything to say about the presence of God, it tells us this: God is to be found in his Word when we accept it in trust, having faith in the Word of a just and loving God which can enable us to share some of that justice and love if we permit. This ability to find God in the Word is perhaps especially evident when the Word is a hard one for us—hard to believe or hard to execute. The very difficulty can be a sign; God's Word brings us to him, but he is always something other than what we expect and as strange and difficult as the unexpected, the strange, usually is. It must be so when the otherness is total, as it is in God. But it is in meeting God, even though it be difficult, that we are saved. Ultimately the prophets teach us (e.g., Ezek. 34, 11-16) that the difficulty is but a passing moment, and that God in his union with his people confers a peace and security beyond our imagining.

Josef Schreiner/*Münster, West Germany*

# Sin as the Cause of Man's Turning Away from God

The nearness of God, which Old Testament preachers, prophets and priests strove mightily to make into an enduring reality, is a freely proffered gift. Yahweh grants it when, where and to whom he wills. When he chose Zion as his dwelling place (Ps. 132, 13) so that he might be present in the midst of his people (Lev. 26, 11; Jer. 14, 9), this was a gratuitous act on his part. Men cannot ensure his presence with buildings and institutions; even in the temple God's presence is an ever new gift of his nearness.[1] The Lord is always both near and distant (cf. Jer. 23, 23), a self-revealing God (Ps. 76, 2) and a hidden God (Is. 45, 15).

Yahweh is ever in a position to abandon the place where he is present, to deprive his people of his sight (Jer. 1 and 7), or to move away from them (Ezek. 10, 18ff.). Jesus Christ, who is greater than the temple (Mt. 12, 6), became the locus of God's presence in accordance with the divine plan of salvation; yet God's nearness still remains something that is at God's free disposal. The Father grants the kingdom and sonship to those whom he has elected.[2] Even when God does mercifully grant us his presence, we do not possess it with absolute and permanent

---

[1] This is made clear in Nathan's words (2 Sam. 7, 5-7); see J. Schreiner, *Sion-Jerusalem:Jahwes Königssitz* (Munich, 1957), pp. 89ff.

[2] See Lk. 12, 32; 14, 15; 22, 28ff.; Jn. 1, 12; 17, 2.

certainty. It is not jeopardized by God, of course, for he keeps his word, stands by his promises, and does not renege on his wish to save all men. God's presence is jeopardized by man's behavior, as the experience of God's people and our own natural feelings suggest. Its reality and perdurance are challenged and threatened by sin.

This article will try to sketch briefly how the Old Testament viewed this problem, and what solution God's Word offered. It does not purport to be a full presentation of this whole question, but merely an attempt to clarify one aspect of the Bible's teaching of sin.

## I

### THE CHIEF TERMS AND THEIR BASIC MEANINGS

Israel did not make a deliberate effort to ponder the nature of sin, to discuss the question in theoretical terms, or to formulate a unified theological presentation. In their journey through history with God or against him, the people of Yahweh discovered experientially about sinfulness and the state of sin. Sin was described as an action of man and a condition of human existence. Thus "Israel used a wide variety of concepts to express its understanding of sinfulness",[3] and it used them to describe the full scope of evil action.[4]

But the people of the Old Testament also used certain words which expressed their evaluation and judgment of sinful actions. The three main words were *hatta't, pasa'* and *'awon*.[5] None of these words was strictly and purely theological, for all of them

[3] G. von Rad, *Theologie des Alten Testaments* I (Munich, 1958), p. 261.

[4] For more on the terminology, see E. Beaucamp, "Péché: I. Dans l'Ancien Testament," in *Dict. de la Bible Suppl.* VII (Paris, 1966), pp. 407-71.

[5] Their connotations are discussed in various "theologies of the Old Testament" and the pertinent biblical and theological lexicons. See, in particular, R. Knieriem, *Die Hauptbegriffe für Sünde im Alten Testament* (Gütersloh, 1965).

came from the sphere of everyday usage and had a secular meaning. This fact prevents us from translating them all with the simple word "sin".

As in the case of many theological concepts in the Old Testament, we can and indeed must delve into the exact meaning of these terms. Only when we examine and understand the secular meaning of these terms will we see how and why the Israelites of the Old Testament regarded a sinful act as worthy of condemnation.

The basic meaning of the stem *ht'* is "to miss the mark" or "fail" (where one shouldn't): "Included in this total were seven hundred picked men who were left-handed, every one of them able to sling a stone at a hair *without missing*" (Jgs. 20, 16). The word was carried over to the sphere of interpersonal relations, where it designated a failure in some relationship that should have been maintained. For example, Jephthah rebukes the Ammonites and asserts that he has never broken their mutual agreement (Jgs. 11, 27), and David asserts that he has always remained a loyal subject of Saul [6] while Shimei accuses him of doing just the opposite (2 Sam. 16, 7; 19, 21).

This meaning remains in theological contexts. Failing Yahweh [7] means not maintaining the relationship that the Lord graciously established between himself and his people. The relationship is broken when Israel worships false gods [8] or uses a graven image to worship Yahweh.[9] It is impugned when the people reject God's leadership (Dt. 1, 41) or disregard his clearly expressed will. Divine worship is off the mark when it involves a form of worship that the Lord does not want,[10] or when the people withhold what is due to him.[11] Their relationship with God is also damaged when they do not maintain

[6] 1 Sam. 24, 11; 26, 21; 19, 4f.

[7] *ht' leyhwh:* Num. 32, 23; Dt. 9, 16; 20, 18; 1 Sam. 7, 6; Jer. 8, 14; *passim.*

[8] See Dt. 20, 18; Jgs. 10, 10. 15; 1 Sam. 7, 6; 12, 10; Jer. 3, 25.

[9] Ex. 32, 30; Dt. 9, 16. 18; Jeroboam's sin in 1 Kgs. 14, 16 and elsewhere.

[10] 1 Sam. 2, 17; 14, 23f.; Mi. 1, 5; Hos. 4, 7.

[11] On vows, see Dt. 23, 22f.; on goods under ban, see Jos. 7, 20.

the proper relationship with their fellow men. Thus we have sinful failing (*hatta't*) when man's actions and conduct challenge or disregard the requirements involved in a properly maintained relationship with God.

This is brought into sharper focus by the second word, *pasa'*. In the secular realm it designates the abolition of a close relationship or the refusal to accept dependency on another. Thus Israel separates from the house of David (1 Kgs. 12, 19), and the same action is taken by Moab [12] and Edom (2 Kgs. 8, 20, 22). Jacob must point out that he has not broken with Laban (Gen. 31, 36ff.), and Abigail hastens to restore good relations with David in order to preclude an imminent break (1 Sam. 25). This same basic meaning is reflected in Amos 1 and 2, where the prophet accuses the nations of damaging community ties by various misdeeds.

The word also has theological underpinnings. Yahweh, the Lord of the world, punishes these misdeeds because he views them as a violation of his dominion and lordship. It is Israel who is primarily responsible for maintaining and observing his rule. The Israelites break with their God when they spurn his counsels, disobey his commandments, run after false gods (Am. 2, 4), flee from their God (Hos. 7, 13), or allow the poor and the blameless to suffer injustice (Am. 2, 7; 5, 12). But every attitude or action which goes against the God-man relationship is basically a falling away from Yahweh and a rupture of this relationship. Thus this word, like the previous one, is frequently used in a general way to designate such actions and attitudes. Sin is really a distortion or perversion of the communal relationship that God would like to see established between himself and man. [13]

This notion finds concrete expression in the word *'awon*. Such perversity marks the conduct of the Sodomites (Gen. 19, 5), the sons of Heli (1 Sam. 3, 13), and even Saul (1 Sam. 20, 1). Human arrogance (Hos. 5, 5) and idolatry (Ezek. 14,

---

[12] 2 Kgs. 1, 1; 3, 5. 7.
[13] R. Knieriem, *op. cit.*, p. 238.

3f.) distort the true state of affairs. People act perversely when they do not look to God and his plan, and when they do not commit themselves to it (Is. 22, 14). In short, every evil act that does not fit in with the proper relationship to God is a distortion, and the word *'awon* is used in this general sense.

Failing to maintain the proper relationship to God and distorting its nature, man stands guilty before God. He has not given God his due. In legal terms he is now a culprit (*rasa*), quite different from the righteous man (*saddiq*) who maintains the proper relationship with God.[14] Sin diminishes or destroys community with God, and man's guilt derives from the fact that his actions and overall behavior do not jibe with the proper God-man relationship. Isaiah berates the people for this fault: "It is your crimes that separate you from your God; it is your sins that make him hide his face so that he will not hear you" (Is. 59, 2). And the people themselves confess their guilt: "That is why right is far from us and justice does not reach us" (Is. 59, 9).

## II
### SIN AS MAN'S DESIRE FOR TOTAL SELF-AUTONOMY

In recognizing that sin is a failure or a distortion in man's relationship to God, the Hebrews established the factual state of affairs and its effects. But the underlying ground of sinful activity had not yet been laid bare. The Israelites pondered the many and varied inducements that led to sin, discovering them in the recollection of their past history and in the admonitions of contemporary prophets. In their prayers to Yahweh they acknowledged these things.

The people of God also tried to pinpoint the ultimate roots of sin, and no one set forth this question more explicitly than the Yahwist author of Genesis.[15] In a narrative story, he sought

[14] See H. Boecker, *Redeformen des Rechtslebens im Alten Testament* (Neukirchen, 1964), p. 135.

[15] See N. Lohfink, "Die Erzählung vom Sündenfall," in *Das Siegeslied am Schilfmeer* (Frankfurt, ²1964), pp. 81-101.

to discover the origins of evil in this world. The creation account in Genesis seeks to provide an answer to this burning question. Occupying the foreground is the story of the fall of our first parents, which the author used to clarify the problem he faced. Starting from his own day and using the heritage of Israel's religious beliefs, he drew up the basic lines of theological thought and then wove them into his story. He was able to do this because he could make use of primitive mythological images and explain them in terms of Israel's faith.

Living around the time of David and Solomon, the Yahwist writer knew that Yahweh had indeed given his people the beautiful land that he had promised them. He was familiar with the basic commandment that dominated Israel since the exodus: to serve Yahweh alone. He also knew that Israelites had once lived miserably in Egypt, and that Yahweh had brought them into health and prosperity. To him the prosperous conditions of his own day were God's blessing (see Gen. 12, 1-3), and they would last only so long as the people maintained their relationship to Yahweh. Yet even amid this happy state of national prosperity, much calamity pervaded human life and cursed its course: sickness, suffering, poverty, community disorder, proclivity toward evil, and death. The Yahwist writer asked himself about the root cause and source of this calamitous state of affairs.

Utilizing some of the basic ideas in Israel's conception of faith (e.g., deliverance into the promised land, God's law, happiness as a reward for its observance), the Yahwist formulated the following line of theological thought: The present unhappy state of affairs, which goes back in time as far as man can remember, resulted from man's violation of some command that God had given him when he was still in a state of happiness. Created in some wilderness, man was transported by God into a paradise. He was given a commandment, and he was blessed with God's nearness in paradise when he observed it. But then man sinned, and all the cursed evils, including death, descended on mankind and there remained up to the Yahwist's own time.

This line of thought uncovered the source of evil. It did not reside in Yahweh, who only does good, nor in the nature of man, who is composed of earth and a divine breath of life.[16] It resided in man's actions. It was also clear that man's sinful action resulted in the breakup of his fellowship with God, as shown by the fact that the first human beings were driven out of the garden of paradise.

The Yahwist author probed even deeper into the mystery of sin. He was able to tell us that man's fellowship with God was dissolved as the result of an act of disobedience, but he wanted to say more. It was not just a question of breaking some whimsical command laid down as a test—e.g., eating forbidden fruit. Israel's religious tradition spoke about a basic commandment upon which the maintenance of divine fellowship depended. The Yahwist argues from this basic commandment, but we can only deduce *a posteriori* what he regarded it to be. In Genesis 3, 5 we read that man wanted to "know good and evil". In Old Testament usage, knowing good and evil meant knowing all things; man, in other words, wanted to have an all-embracing knowledge of everything and to be able to apply this knowledge in shaping his life and the world, even though only God can really have such knowledge.[17] Fusing the image of the tree of knowledge with the old image of the tree of life, the Yahwist seeks to tell us that our first parents wanted to have full control over life and the future; they wanted to have no need for God. By their sinful action, they rebelled against the basic commandment that underlies human existence, the obligation to recognize God as the Lord, and they renounced their dependency relationship with him.

Man's fellowship with God is broken by sin insofar as man tries to be totally autonomous and independent of God. This drama is replayed when men seek to ensure their autonomy and permanence by storming the gates of heaven (Gen.

---

[16] N. Lohfink (*ibid.*, pp. 86f.) rightly points out that here the author precludes pagan conceptions of the *enuma elish*.

[17] On this expression and its meaning, see G. von Rad, *Das erste Buch Mose: Genesis* (Göttingen, 1953), pp. 71f.

11). As the Elohist writer accurately notes, it is replayed wherever fear of the Lord is missing (Gen. 20, 11).[18] For in such cases fellowship with God means nothing to man, and he shows it by his actions.

### III

#### SIN AS A TURNING AWAY FROM GOD

As we have just seen, the sinful aspect of evildoing is man's desire to be totally autonomous and self-sufficient. It disrupts his relationship with God, breaks off contact between them, and destroys their fellowship. Man turns away from God, giving up God's presence and nearness.

Deuteronomic theology was particularly concerned about focusing attention on this fact. It never tired of pointing to man's turning away from Yahweh as the root of all evil. Even before the Deuteronomic age, Hosea (Hos. 4, 10) and Isaiah (Is. 4, 10) had reproached the Israelites for leaving Yahweh, and Jeremiah reproached them even more sharply (Jer. 2, 17ff.). But when the exiled Israelites took a backward look at their past history, it became frighteningly clear how badly their fellowship with God had been disrupted by their betrayal of him and their recourse to other gods (Jgs. 2, 12f. and *passim*).[19]

The prophets had been right: "Your own wickedness chastises you, your own infidelities punish you. Know then and see how evil and bitter are your forsaking the Lord, your God, and showing no fear of me" (Jer. 2, 19). The admonitions of Hosea (Hos. 2, 15) and Deuteronomy (Dt. 6, 12; 8, 11) had been in vain, for the Israelites did forget their God (Jgs. 3, 7; 1 Sam. 12, 9) and turn away from him (Jer. 32, 40).

Yahweh was provoked to anger by his people's worship of false gods (Jgs. 2, 12; 1 Kgs. 14, 15). He had every right to

[18] See H. Wolff, "Zur Thematik der elohistischen Fragmente im Pentateuch," in *Ev. Theol.* 27 (1969), pp. 59-72.

[19] In order not to overload the footnotes, only a few scriptural citations will be given in the following notes.

question their conduct: "What fault did your fathers find in men that they withdrew from me, went after empty idols, and became empty themselves?" (Jer. 2, 5). Israel could give no answer to this question. God had planned to adopt Israel as his child, and to give it a fair and prosperous land. He thought that the Israelites would call him "Father" and not turn away from him, but they proved to be unfaithful (Jer. 2, 20).

What did this turning away from Yahweh involve, according to the Deuteronomic viewpoint? It involved the Israelites' departure from the path which the Lord had shown them through his law (Dt. 5, 32; 9, 12. 16), and their recourse to other gods (Dt. 6, 14; 8, 19). It involved the abandonment of the commandments (1 Kgs. 18, 8) and the covenant which he had established (Dt. 29, 24). It shows up in their refusal to hear his voice (Dt. 8, 20; 9, 23), their rejection of his counsels (Am. 2, 4), and their forgetfulness of the covenant (Hos. 4, 6). In general, it shows up whenever the people do what is evil in Yahweh's sight (Num. 32, 13 and *passim*).

The sin of God's people is turning away from Yahweh. It could be described in the aforementioned terms, or by such terms as rebellion (Is. 1, 20), breaking of the covenant (Jgs. 2, 20; Dt. 31, 10. 16), haughtiness (Is. 2), stiff-neckedness (Ex. 32, 9) and infidelity (Jer. 3, 8. 11. 20). By turning away from God, they broke the basic obligation imposed on them. They disregarded the command to have no other gods and to worship Yahweh with their whole heart and soul.[20] Only fulfillment of this basic command makes it possible for man to have real fellowship with God. The people of Yahweh were forced to acknowledge their guilt: "Yes, our offenses are present to us and our crimes we know: Transgressing and denying the Lord, turning back from following our God, threatening outrage and apostasy, uttering words of falsehood the heart has conceived" (Is. 59, 13).

[20] See N. Lohfink, *Höre Israel: Auslegung von Texten aus dem Buch Deuteronomium* (Düsseldorf, 1965).

## IV
### SIN AS A FAILING IN HUMAN FELLOWSHIP

From what we have said it might seem that the Old Testament saw sin only when man turned directly against God and refused to serve him. But this is certainly not the case. The prophets clearly pointed out that God also saw sin when man injured his fellow men or disrupted human fellowship.[21]

It is easy enough to see that interpersonal misdemeanors represent an injustice against one's fellow men. But to what extent are they to be regarded as violations of the God-man relationship? Why are they sins? To be sure, the Lord had expressly forbidden such acts, as the decalogue and the Mosaic law indicate. If a person committed such acts, he was transgressing God's expressed will and the rules of fellowship that he had laid down. But in the Old Testament view, the sinfulness of these interpersonal transgressions did not reside solely in the breaking of God's commandment. There was an even deeper motif.

Yahweh's covenant was, first and foremost, with his chosen people as such, not with the individual. He established a relationship with the nation, and only consequently with each individual who belonged to that nation. Conversely, anyone who entered a relationship with Yahweh necessarily belonged to the "community of the Lord", which arose and perdured only because it had a relationship with Yahweh. The relationship of each individual to Yahweh was tied up with God's covenant nation. Thus, if a person damaged the fellowship and community of God's people by an unjust act, he simultaneously transgressed the relationship with God that he had been granted. He sinned in two dimensions, injuring his fellow man and turning away from God.

21 For example: Am. 1, 3—2, 8; 4, 1; 5, 10; Is. 5; Mi. 2; Jer. 7.

A similar situation existed with humanity as a whole. Through God's act of creation, as the Yahwist indicated in his creation account, the human race constitutes one big family. Under his lordship, it forms a many-branched community of nations despite all the differences that exist between peoples. Whenever a person rises up against others (Gen. 4), he attacks the Lord and creator as well. This point gets special stress in the priestly account. It is basically the same failing we found in the account of man's fall. Man thereby turns against God and offends against the prescribed relationship with his Lord. It is highly significant that the Yahwist writer puts the story of Cain right after the account of man's fall. At a very early stage, God's people recognized and acknowledged what the surrounding nations also knew—namely that an offense against a human being is also a sin against God.

## V

### SINFUL ACTS AND THEIR CONSEQUENCES

Sin, as a turning away from God, was more than a passing act of the moment. It transposed the sinner from nearness to God to distance from him, from saving contact with God to damning loss of contact, from fellowship with God to separation from God. It brought about a perduring condition in which the former relationship with God was destroyed. That was the dangerous and oppressive result which sin produced.

This state of affairs was summed up in the notion that God had turned his face away from the sinner, and that the latter now lived in a state of hopelessness. However, more than this was involved. God, who once had created and maintained a happy relationship with man, was now angered and vexed. He responded with angry invective and threatened punishment. His people could not remain long in doubt about this fact. From the very beginning God had made this clear by word and deed. The whole matter was clearly set forth in their covenant obligations (Dt. 28), and it was confirmed over and over again by Israel's history.

The prophets and the historical books pointed up the disastrous consequences of sin in the events of history. They pointed particularly to the annihilation of the Northern and Southern Kingdoms and to the destruction of Jerusalem. When Yahweh abandoned his people, he surrendered them to punishment and catastrophe.

But the case was not always clear when misfortune struck. Was it always to be regarded as a punishment from God? Had the people committed some sin of which they were unaware? The Israelites were fully aware of this problem, and they were concerned about it.[22] In the early days they believed that their relationship with God could be broken by unconscious failings. Balaam believed this to be the case (Num. 22, 34), the psalmist attributed his sickness to some sin (Pss. 38, 4. 19; 41, 4), and the ritual code prescribed rites for such instances (Lev. 4—5; Num. 15, 25ff.). The Elohist writer sought to come to grips with this problem, suggesting that God secretly keeps man from sinning, or enables him to make a conscious decision, or shows him how to avert such consequences (Gen. 20). It is only with Ezekiel, however, that the responsibility of the individual finds clear expression (Ezek. 18, 33) and brings us closer to a solution of the problem.

But every time Israel's relationship with God was disturbed by some conscious or unconscious failing, those affected had to ask themselves whether or not the old ties could be restored. For neither the individual nor the nation could live without God or in opposition to him. Separation from him meant misery and eventual death.[28] Unless the relationship with God was reestablished, the sinner was lost. But here there was a dilemma which had to be faced: "If one man shall sin against

[22] See W. Eichrodt, *Theologie des Alten Testaments* II/III (Stuttgart-Göttingen, ⁴1961), pp. 264ff.; J. Hempel, *Das Ethos des Alten Testaments* (1938), pp. 52ff.

[28] This conception is visible already in Genesis 3, and it appears as a shadowy backdrop in Deuteronomy 28; 29, 19; 30, 15-18.

another, God may be appeased in his behalf; but if a man shall sin against the Lord, who shall pray for him?" (1 Sam. 2, 25).

## VI
### RESTORING FELLOWSHIP WITH GOD

The Israelites were able to answer this question of Heli in a positive way. Their early history had taught them that the Lord wants to save men. In his account of salvation history the Yahwist writer shows us that God reestablished fellowship with man anew in Noah and Abraham, despite man's rebellion and apostasy. From the experience of his own marriage, Hosea tells us that Yahweh is not going to abandon faithless Israel; rather, he is working to restore the covenant relationship (Hos. 1—3). Jeremiah picks up this image (2—4) and reiterates God's offer. Even though the people have broken the covenant, the Lord will stand by them, renewing their relationship in a new covenant that will deepen the tie and make it possible for man to remain faithful (Jer. 31, 31-34). Even after the nation's sins have forced Yahweh to make the break apparent by abandoning the temple and moving away from his people, he is still prepared to return to them and to offer his presence once again (Ezek. 43).

On a purely rational level God's conduct is difficult to understand, as Hosea saw. Even God himself muses about it: "How could I give you up, O Ephraim, or deliver you up, O Israel? . . . My heart is overwhelmed, my pity stirred . . . for I am God and not man" (Hos. 11, 8-9). It is God's unconditioned and unaccountable love at work. The Lord appears to his people from afar, shows them mercy from age to age (Jer. 31, 3), and does not forget them (Is. 49, 14ff.). Pardon and forgiveness emanate from his nearby presence, prompting him to forgive sin and to heal the rift caused by infidelity.[24] Yahweh takes

[24] On the vocabulary and its meaning, see J. Stamm, *Erlösen und Vergeben im Alten Testament* (Bern, 1940); E. Beaucamp, *op. cit.*, pp.

away sin (Mic. 7, 18; 32, 1) and sets it aside. He allows sin and its effects to be shunted aside (2 Sam. 12, 13) from the guilty party. He wipes the slate clean (Is. 44, 21f.) and washes sin away (Ps. 51, 3. 9), so that man is purified. God casts sin far away (Ps. 103, 12) and hurls it into the depths of the sea (Mic. 7, 9). He thinks no more about it (Jer. 31, 34) and does not impute it to the sinner (Ps. 32, 2). As the priestly viewpoint puts it, he "covers" sin and heals the wounds in the fellowship between himself and man (Hos. 6, 10f.). All these images say the same thing: God forgives (Ex. 34, 9). His readiness to forgive is buried in Israel's talk about God's mercy, grace, help, fidelity and redemption.

But let there be no misunderstanding here. Yahweh does not take sin lightly, nor does he forgive indiscriminately. Joshua does not hesitate to say that "he is a jealous God who will not forgive your transgressions or your sins" (Jos. 24, 19). The Israelites' experience taught them two things about Yahweh: he is ready to forgive (Is. 1, 14), but he can also refuse to give forgiveness (2 Kgs. 24, 4). Their praise of him will acknowledge both facts: "The Lord, the Lord, a merciful and gracious God, slow to anger and rich in kindness and fidelity, continuing his kindness for a thousand generations, and forgiving wickedness and crime and sin, yet not declaring the guilty guiltless. . . ." (Ex. 34, 6-7). God's mercy and forgiveness are highlighted in this hymn of praise. He is ever ready to restore contact, but not without the cooperation of man who has moved away from him.

## VII

### OBLIGATIONS OF THE SINNER

When the Lord restores his merciful presence, he does this without any prior work on man's part. But the shattered ties

---

464-69; P. van Imschoot, *Theologie de l'Ancien Testament* II (Paris, 1956), pp. 333-38.

of fellowship can only be mended if certain preconditions are met. The sinner has given up his attachment to God and rejected his presence. In thought and deed he must now show that he would like to change this state of affairs.

The first requirement is an awareness of the situation he has brought about and an admission of his sinful guilt: "Ah, Lord, great and awesome God, you who keep your merciful covenant toward those who love you and observe your commandments! We have sinned, been wicked and done evil: we have rebelled and departed from your commandments and your laws" (Dn. 9, 4-5). Right, of course, stands on the Lord's side, and it is for him to grant pardon or refuse it. But man can hope in God's merciful forgiveness.

Confession of guilt and pleas for forgiveness are not enough. If a man has turned away from God, he must return to him once again. That is the requirement pronounced repeatedly by the prophets. The call to conversion is sounded from the days of Amos to those of Malachi. It is stressed by Hosea and becomes a central theme for Jeremiah.[25] It summons man to "return to his original relationship with Yahweh",[26] reminding him that "God's loving counsel does not abandon the sinner to his fate".[27]

Conversion becomes a reality when man abandons his evil ways (Ezek. 18, 23) and reforms his deeds (Jer. 7, 3). He can then turn back to the Lord, who will restore fellowship with him (Jer. 3, 22; 4, 1). For God does not wish the death of the sinner; he wants him to undergo conversion and live (Ezek. 33, 11). It is this merciful Word of God that offers hope to the sinner and a future in God's presence.

[25] See H. Wolff, "Das Thema 'Umkehr' in der alttestamentlichen Prophetie," in *Gesammelte Studien zum Alten Testament* (Munich, 1964), pp. 130-50; G. Fohrer, "Umkehr und Erlösung beim Propheten Hosea," in *Studien zur alttestamentlichen Prophetie* (Berlin, 1967), pp. 222-41.
[26] H. Wolff, *op. cit.*, p. 135.
[27] G. Fohrer, *op. cit.*, p. 241.

Chrysostome Larcher, O.P./*Saint-Boil, France*

# Divine Transcendence as Another Reason for God's Absence

## I
### ANCIENT MAN AND DIVINE TRANSCENDENCE

Awareness of a difference in nature or mode of existence between man and the divinity aroused widely varying reactions in the world of antiquity. Relying on his natural passions, tendencies or conceptions, ancient man reacted to bring the divine world close to him, or to move it as far away as possible. He could experience the sense of the sacred in a striking or even terrifying way, feeling the awesome presence of divinity. He could also render the divine innocuous by enshrining it in external rites, or even regard it as ineffectual on the terrestrial level.

God's absence is felt as a real absence only when man believes in the possibility of his intervention and is surprised by his silence and inaction. In the world of the Sumerians and Babylonians, the pressing question of the conduct and intentions of the gods surfaced in the lament of the "suffering just man",[1] and it finds cogent expression in the dramatic monologue entitled "I shall praise the Lord of Wisdom": [2]

[1] See S. Kramer, "Man and His God," in *Supplements to the Vetus Testamentum* III (Leiden, 1955), pp. 170-82; J. Nougavrol, "Une version ancienne du 'Juste souffrant'," in *RB* (1952), pp. 239-50.

[2] Full text in *Ancient Near Eastern Texts Relating to the Old Testament,* ed. by J. Pritchard (Princeton, 1950), pp. 434-37.

49

Who can know the will of the gods in heaven?
The counsels of the infernal gods, who can understand
them?
How could man possibly learn the ways of a god?

For the Greek world we have the celebrated verse of Theognis
(382-381 B.C.):

There is no code established by the gods for man,
No path marked out to show us how to please the immortal
ones.

The men of the Old Testament followed an analogous line
of thought, but there was one difference—namely that divine
revelation intervened to accentuate or profoundly modify their
spontaneous natural reactions. In particular, the ancient
Semitic notion of holiness was transposed to Yahweh, designat-
ing the one who was distinct by nature from everything created
and who could not tolerate human sin. Undoubtedly associated
with this idea was the equally ancient notion that man could
not look on God (Ex. 19, 21; 33, 20; Lv. 16, 2; Jgs. 6, 22-23;
Is. 6, 5) or hear him (Dt. 4, 33; 5, 24; Ex. 20, 19) without
dying. To be sure, the Old Testament also presents experiences
of a totally opposite nature (Ex. 24, 10-11; 33, 11; Dt. 34,
10; Is. 6, 1. 5), but it always underlines the exceptional nature
of such experiences (Ex. 20, 19; 24, 16; 33, 16-23; 34, 6-9).
    In different ways revelation reinforced the mystery of the God
of the covenant. He is a God who lives alone, and who cannot
be depicted by any graven image. Revelation also stressed his
oneness and uniqueness. This long process, marked by a
series of prophetic interventions, culminated in a quasi-gospel
of divine transcendence in Deutero-Isaiah.

## Deutero-Isaiah and Divine Transcendence

Yahweh is the unique being who has no rival. All our conceptions of the divine fade away before him (43, 10-13; 44,

7-8; 45, 5-6. 14). He is the incomparable one because no earthly image can depict him (40, 18. 25; 46, 5). In the beginning he created everything, "naming" or "calling" them into existence (40, 12. 22. 26; 44, 24; 45, 12. 18), and all his creatures continue to obey his summons (40, 26; 44, 26-28) and his Word (55, 11) because his creative activity goes on effortlessly (40, 28) and extends to all things (45, 7).

Yahweh is an eternal God (40, 28) who rules time; he is both "the first" and "the last" (41, 4; 44, 6; 48, 12). In contrast with the divinities that are bound up with astrological determinism (47, 13), Yahweh is sovereignly free (45, 9-12). He can intervene in history in some unforeseeable way, even when he has proclaimed this intervention well ahead of time (41, 22-23. 26-27; 43, 9; 44, 7; 45, 21; 46, 10; 48, 3-7). He is the "creator" in the very bosom of history (41, 20; 43, 7; 45, 8; 48, 7). His mind cannot be sounded (40, 28), nor do his thoughts have anything in common with those of man (40, 13-14; 55, 8-9). No outside pressure can be brought to bear on him, and he keeps his own counsels (48, 9-11).

Finally, Yahweh is a holy God (43, 15), separated from everything created by his very nature and totally opposed to the sins of man. But this holiness no longer creates an unbridgeable chasm between God and man; instead it creates new links between them, and it is associated intimately with other attributes. It involves election (cf. 43, 3; 45, 11; etc.). It is suffused with pity, mercy (40, 2; 43, 22-28; 48, 4. 8-10), and tenderness (43, 1-7; 49, 14ff.; 54, 4-10). The "holy one of Israel" becomes her redeemer (41, 14; 54, 5) or her savior (43, 3). He himself will come to deliver her (40, 3-5. 9-11). He will be close to her or "with her" (41, 10; 43, 2. 5), and the nations will be forced to acknowledge that a "hidden God" (45, 15) resides with her.

The message of Deutero-Isaiah appeals to faith. Instead of tackling the difficulties of the exiled Israelites, Deutero-Isaiah calls for unreserved faith in the one, incomparable God who will eventually come to save Israel. He directly envisions a specific people, although there are certain universalist overtones in his message (cf. 45, 20-24). His attention remains fixed on Israel as a collectivity, not on individuals as such.

### The Individual and Divine Transcendence

By contrast, the book of Job deals with the problem of an individual and seems to have no interest in the collective destiny of God's people. It embodies a literary genre where experience plays a preponderant role and where reflection on the human condition results in posing some agonizing questions to God. The author of this poetic dialogue begins by recounting the edifying story of Job and his patience in adversity. He then goes on to initiate a long debate in which Job recounts his unmerited suffering to God, appeals to his fidelity and justice, and pleads the cause of all hapless men before him. Both God and man gain stature in this debate, for the poet-author has no intention of sacrificing one for the sake of the other.

The biblical notion of man is presupposed throughout. In 7, 17-18 Job himself ironically picks up the words of Psalm 8, 5-7, which hearken back to Genesis 1, 26-28. But their scope is broadened in a curious way. Far from feeling happy over his fate, man is an unsatisfied being. At the end of a life that is all too brief and torturous (14, 1-2), man disappears forever. For man, death is the end of everything (14, 7-12); it extinguishes his hope of happiness (7, 6-7; 14, 7. 19; 17, 15; 21, 25), leaves his desire for justice unsatisfied (cf. 19, 23-27), and interrupts the friendship he has struck up with God (7, 8; 14, 14-15). Subject to disappointment and deception always, man would be better off if he had never existed or if he disappeared quickly without a trace (3, 1-23; 10, 18-19).

We then tune in on a long plea where man recalls his dignity (10, 8-12), his need for autonomy (10, 13-14. 20; 14, 6), and his longing to be understood, respected, heard and even loved by God; after all, God should love his creature, for he needs him (cf. 7, 8. 21; 14, 15; 19, 26-27). But the immediate cause of Job's plea is the unjustified suffering that now oppresses him. He stands alone before God, supported only by the testimony of his conscience. He has absolute faith in a unique, personal God who has created everything (9, 8-10) and exercises complete control over this creation (9, 5-7. 24; 12, 7. 10. 14-25; etc.). It is a very pure and spiritual faith, totally disengaged from material rites.

To defend the law of temporal retribution and to vindicate God's justice, the three interlocutors seek to make Job aware of some fault. They talk about warnings, salutary corrections, and chastisement for open or secret sins. Job refuses to get involved in this train of thought, and in desperation he turns to God. He wants to talk it over with God, to plead his case and defend his rights, to find out if there is some other reason behind his misfortune. But Job does not know how to reach this mysterious God who lives and acts on another plane and seems to have no regard for human considerations. Distressed, exasperated and shattered, Job begins to question God's goodness, loyalty and justice toward man. He becomes the spokesman for all those who, like him, are disappointed by life (3, 20-23) or oppressed unjustly (9, 22-24; 12, 6; 24, 1-12). Events take place in the world as if God did not control or govern anything, or as if he were completely indifferent to good and evil (21, 7-35; 24, 1-17). Is God a laggardly shirker, wholly occupied with unimportant things (7, 20-21; 9, 29-31; 10, 4; 13, 23-28; 14, 3-4)? Or is he a cruel, vindictive God, solely concerned with his own rights and totally insensitive to human suffering (7, 12-14; 9, 13. 17-18; 10, 15-17; 16, 12-14; 19, 6-12; 30, 18. 21-22)?

These musings are strong enough to evoke violent proposals in Job's mind, but they do not destroy his faith in a good and faithful God who should respect the testimony of a human conscience. This dialogue ends with Job's challenge to God (31, 35-37). Strangely enough, Job's titanic inner struggle accentuates certain aspects of God's transcendence. God, responsible for everything and at work in everything, lies wholly beyond human reach. He remains imperceptible and intangible. He acts out of total freedom, and cannot be programmed in advance. His ways are not rational, and there exists between man and him a chasm that only such faith as Job's can bridge. But Job's faith, in turn, seeks some guarantee or sign. In some obscure way, it calls for an arbitrator or mediator between God and man (cf. 9, 33-34; 16, 18-27; 19, 25-27).

The interlocutors, too, bring up God's transcendence. God is the holy one who tolerates no evil (4, 17-18; 11, 7-9; 15, 14-16; 25, 4-6). Residing in the lofty heights of heaven (22, 12), he is the all-powerful creator and the invincible sovereign (25, 2) who has triumphed over the forces of chaos (26, 12-13). This transcendence, now encased in clear-cut categories and rendered somehow static, becomes something reassuring for the just. They know the norms of providence and its ways of governing. Justice is always recompensed here below, and the apparent exceptions prove the rule because they can be explained as warnings, corrections, or summonses to humility. If man lives justly, he should feel contented with his lot and look for nothing more.

In reality, the three interlocutors have lost sight of the mysteriousness of God, if not of his real nature. Moreover, their attitude toward man is rigidly frozen and they can no longer feel compassion for those who are struck with misfortune. To them death seems to be the normal culmination of a happy life (cf. 5, 26), while Job reacts strongly against its abnormal and horrifying character. In the last analysis, they no longer see the need for a mediator between God and man (cf. 5, 1. 8).

God's intervention (38—42) relaxes the tension created by the dialogue, but it does not resolve the problem posed. God replies to Job from the depths of his transcendence (38, 1), challenging him with the spectacle of creation. The power and intelligence that organized the world, and the wisdom that still is at work in the universe, are enough to confound man and convince him of his limitations. Moreover, the whole spectacle of nature is merely a reflection of God's ways in history, for there he deploys the same superior power, wisdom, and sovereignity. In summoning God to justify his attitude, Job has somehow set himself up as his rival. Instead, he should follow the example of his creator,[3] using his power and intelligence to diminish or conquer evil (40, 2-14). On an even deeper level, Job is reminded that he is a simple creature, and he is invited to purify his faith by abandoning himself totally to the mystery of God. Faith thus becomes trusting acceptance of this mystery and the renunciation of narrow-minded, superficial attitudes.

Through some sort of illumination that contrasts sharply with the teaching of his interlocutors and his own natural reactions (42, 5), Job perceives the absolute transcendence of God. Accepting this transcendence and submitting to it, he comes out of his trial purified, and by renouncing his claim to personal vindication, he is justified. It is this decisive step from revolt to self-abandonment, from refusal to acceptance, that God wanted him to make—without, however, giving an answer to Job's questions.

Looking at the book as a whole, we find that Job's sincerity is approved by God in the epilogue (42, 7-8). His interlocutors, on the other hand, are reproved. To defend God, they went so far as to condemn an innocent man. To save God's transcendence, they would be willing to destroy man. While God's transcendence is a necessary thing that man must accept, it should not prompt him to total submission or to the renunciation of his own conscience and its claims. It simply invites man to plunge himself in a mystery that goes beyond him. To be sure, the book does end on a reassuring note that seems to justify the theory of the three interlocutors. Virtue, it seems, does finally receive its recompense here below. But this reassuring turn of events can no longer dissipate the mal-

[3] Cf. E. Jacob, *Théologie de l'A.T.* (Neuchâtel, 1955), p. 139.

aise produced by the disconcerting questions of the earlier dialogue. The law of temporal retribution is no longer verifiable in human experience.

## II
### RAPPROCHEMENT BETWEEN GOD AND MAN

Alongside these conscious reminders of the distance between God and man, the Old Testament opens up new perspectives of a different sort. In some instances it reminds man of his privileged nature, inviting him to collaborate with God or to draw near to him by imitating him. In other instances, God seems to choose to draw closer and closer to man.

### Man as the Image of God

Created in the "image of God" (Gn. 1, 26-27; 5, 1), man by his very nature is elevated above the animal world. To a certain extent he resembles God (and the *elohim* who form God's court; cf. Ps. 8, 6 and Gn. 3, 22). Here below he is God's visible representative, charged with ruling certain domains of the created universe in God's place (Gn. 1, 26. 28; Ps. 8, 7; Sir. 17, 2-4; Wis. 9, 2-3; 10, 2). Like the creator God of Genesis 1,[4] he is a being who speaks, decides, chooses and commands; he is a free, intelligent being, capable of making his own decisions and taking responsibility for his actions (Gn. 3, 5. 22; Sir. 15, 14; 17, 7). He is a person, not simply an individual creature (cf. Gn. 9, 6).

This natural condition poses a continual problem to man. It obliges him to respect himself and others. It invites him to collaborate with God. Tied up with his mission to govern lower creatures and to exploit the energies of the created world (Wis. 14, 5) is the corresponding duty to be mindful of the creator

[4] Cf. W. Eichrodt, *Theologie des Alten Testaments* II (Leipzig, 1935), p. 61.

(cf. Wis. 13, 1-9) and to avoid abusing other creatures. This condition also obliges him to live in a way that will bring him as close as possible to God. Tied up with his resemblance to God is the corresponding obligation to imitate him. As he is reminded in one context: "Be holy, for I, the Lord, your God, am holy" (Lv. 19, 2).

The Israelite community would reflect God's transcendent holiness. It would be "separated" from other nations, removed from sin, and united by mutual love, so long as each Israelite faithfully observed the whole ensemble of moral and ritual prescriptions (Lv. 19, 3-37).

But the invitation to imitate God takes many other forms in the Old Testament, notably when it proposes as a model Yahweh's activity in history (Dt. 24, 17-22; Lv. 25, 39-43; etc.), his feelings or reactions (Ex. 20, 5; 22, 26; 34, 14; Dt. 25, 16; etc.), and his attributes of justice, fidelity and goodness. Finally, the "image of God" theme takes on a Greek flavor in Wisdom 2, 23, and it is tied up with the privilege of incorruptibility presupposed in the account of Genesis 2—3.

For the author of Wisdom, immortality is always assured to justice (1, 15), and it is based on a reality of nature that is none other than the soul. However, it is not reducible to an exigency of nature. Man must ensure it by works of justice. It introduces him into the company of God, who bestows it as a reward and as a favor. The author of Wisdom discusses man's permanent vocation to immortality in a highly original context: man has been created as a living image of "something that belongs properly to God", that is, his eternity; of his very nature, man retains the capability of actualizing and definitively establishing this image.

The ways in which the transcendent God seems to deliberately draw near to man are many. Two basic types of approach are evident. Sometimes a human being, such as a king or another representative of the people, is elevated to the border of the divine realm. Sometimes divine energies and attributes, at work in the world, tend to become more and more stable and human.

### The Messiah King

Here I do not intend to trace the history of personal messianism in detail. I merely want to highlight the main stages of this history and the successive transformations it underwent.

Nathan assured David that his dynasty would endure forever (2 Sam. 7, 11-16). Several centuries later, Isaiah drew an incomparable portrait of a future king who would sit on the throne of David. In successive strokes he depicts the birth of a wondrous infant who will introduce some sort of permanent divine presence among the "remnant" of Israel; he will do this because he will merit the name Emmanuel, "God with us" (Is. 7, 14; 8, 8. 10).

Other titles seem to elevate this personage above the purely human level (9, 5), for they have divine overtones. (Note the "mighty God" of Is. 10, 21.) He will be inhabited by the Spirit of God (11, 2), who will fill him with wisdom and power. Finally, he will bring about a reign of endless peace in righteousness and justice (9, 6; 11, 5-8), and knowledge of Yahweh will fill the land (11, 9).

This portrait will be enriched with parallel ideas (Mi. 5, 1-2; Ps. 110) and further extensions (Ps. 72). In some points it will be modified by later prophets (Jer. 23, 5; Ezek. 34, 23; 37, 24-25; Zech. 9, 9-10). But all the essentials are set forth by Isaiah, and nowhere else in the Bible does the messianic king, the anointed of Yahweh, appear so close to God and, at the same time, so capable of radiating God's presence in the midst of his purified people.

Gradually, however, these future perspectives would lose their appeal and pointedness. Undoubtedly this was due to the fact that the kings of Israel proved more and more disappointing. The promises and predictions of later prophets would often disregard the intermediary role of the future king, or else they would transform him into a "prince" (Ezek. 37, 25), presiding over a theocracy that God, the true pastor, would govern by stable and definitive institutions.

We also see the introduction of other figures who seem to eclipse the Davidic Messiah. We encounter the suffering servant in Deutero-Isaiah (42, 1-9; 49, 1-9; 50, 4-11; 52, 13—53, 12), and then the Son of Man in the book of Daniel.

## The Suffering Servant

Individual and collective interpretations of the suffering servant continue to vie with one another. I prefer to conciliate the two views. An individual personage becomes the eminent representative of a collective group (the Israelites who remained faithful to God in a time of trial), or he emerges from this group. The royal characteristics of the servant and his points of contact with the messianic king are quite secondary and hardly apparent. In any case, much transposition has occurred. His prophet-like characteristics, with respect to his vocation and his mission, are much more evident.

Yet even these traits are superseded on several points. The mission of the servant relates to pagan peoples, even to the most distant isles (42, 4. 6; 49, 1. 6; 52, 14-15). His undeserved sufferings have expiatory value for the sins of "many" (53, 5-6. 8. 10-12), bringing them "healing" and "peace" (53, 5). Finally, at the end of the period of trial, and only then, he will be given dominion over many peoples (53, 12).

The image of a new Israel, profoundly affected by the dolorous experiences of certain prophets (Jeremiah in particular), takes definite shape in the background. But its chief or master is an eminently religious person whose mission culminates in the voluntary acceptance of humiliation, suffering and death for the salvation of many. The suffering servant is identified with these many, and with the mysterious designs of a saving God. Under this twofold aspect, the servant remains in full solidarity with men, but at the same time be is elevated above them, not only by his piety and his superior knowledge of God but also by his generous collaboration with the divine plan of salvation.

## The Son of Man

The figure of the Son of Man takes shape on a transcendent level from the very first. He comes "on the clouds of heaven", and he presents himself before the "ancient one" to receive dominion over all peoples (Dn. 7, 13-14). Vaguely described as someone "like a son of man", he does not seem to be reducible to a purely human being. That is why some propose to identify him with an angel, or to regard him as the incarnation of divine Glory or divine Wisdom.[5]

On the other hand, we witness an investiture scene which seems to anticipate that of the "holy people of the Most High" (7, 27), because the same sovereignty is promised to them. Moreover, an apocalyptic vision can transpose terrestrial realities to a celestial plane in order to give them deeper significance or to underline their transcendent outcome. Thus the Son of Man could belong primarily, or to some extent, to the terrestrial sphere. It is worth nothing that the "holy ones" receive dominion and empire (7, 23-26) only after they have been persecuted under the dominion of the "fourth beast", and there is a close link between them and the Son of Man, so much so that some readily view him as their eminent representative or chief. Is it possible that he, too, is rewarded munificently only after enduring trials similar to, or identical with, those of the suffering servant?

In any case it seems to me that Daniel stresses the glorification of this mysterious personage, his definitive accession to the divine plane, and his eventual participation in God's own sovereignty over all peoples. Is he also viewed as a superhuman being? The complex associations of the apocalyptic genre make this a real possibility, but we do not know what the determining influence was here. Is it the "divine" aureole of the Messiah

---

[5] Cf. A. Feuillet, "Le Fils de l'homme de Daniel et la tradition biblique," in *RB* (1953), pp. 170-202, 321-46.

prefigured by Isaiah, the Wisdom that is both transcendent and very close to man, or the statement that the mien of the suffering servant was not like that of a son of man (Is. 52, 14)?

## The Word

With the Word, the Spirit, or Wisdom, God draws progressively closer to man. Certain entities that emanate from God and concretize his providential activity become more and more solidly established. They provide assurance of some permanent divine presence, and thus create a link between God and man.

The Word did more than create the world at the beginning (Gn. 1; Ps. 33, 6. 9; Jdt. 16, 14; Wis. 9, 1). It continues to work in nature (Pss. 107, 25; 147, 15. 18; 119, 69; Is. 40, 26; 44, 27; etc.). It is also a Word of revelation, informing Israel of God's wishes. While this Word is more and more fixed in the written law, it remains a living thing for each and every individual (Dt. 30, 11-14; Ps. 119, 103. 140; see also Dt. 8, 3 and Wis. 6, 26). The successive experiences of the prophets—of Jeremiah in particular—show that it is not only a light but also an irresistible force (Dt., 18, 18; Jer. 1, 9ff.; 20, 7-9; 23, 29; etc.). Finally, it is a Word of salvation, intervening to deliver people from peril (2 Kgs, 2, 21-22; Ps. 107, 20; Wis. 16, 12) and to accomplish the will of God through decisive events (Is. 40, 5; 41, 4. 9; 44, 26; etc. ). Its effectiveness is sovereign (Is. 55, 10-11) and irreversible (Is. 40, 8; 45, 23).

## The Spirit

The activity of the Spirit alternates with that of the Word, but it has its own characteristics. One readily attributes to it those divine interventions which surprise men by their suddenness and force, for it is the source of a transcendent energy and comparable to a violent wind. Viewed also as the vital breath of the living God, it becomes a vivifying principle. Perhaps regarded in this light in Genesis 1, 2, it communicates life to every creature (Ps. 104, 29-30; Wis. 12, 1), and especially to man (Gn. 2, 7; Ezek. 37, 5-10; Jb. 27, 3; 33, 4; 34, 14-15).

It is also a supernatural principle of knowledge, perhaps because it is seen as informing or counseling (cf. Is. 40, 13) God's intelligence. It dispenses counsel, prudence, wisdom (Num. 11, 17. 25; 27, 15-18; Dt. 34, 9; Is. 11, 2; Jb. 32, 8), and a wide variety of knowledge (Ex. 28, 3; 31, 3; 35, 31; etc.). More and more as time goes on, prophetic revelations are attributed to it (2 Sam. 23, 2; 2 Kgs. 2, 9. 15; Hos. 9, 7; Ezek. 11, 5; Jl. 3, 1-2; Neh. 9, 30; Zech. 7, 12). Finally, it is a holy Spirit opposed by nature to human sin, because it is the Spirit of the transcendent God. When this aspect is combined with the aforementioned aspects, particularly in a messianic perspective, the Spirit becomes the supreme principle of excellence in man's moral and religious life—after it has purified men from sin (cf. Pss. 51, 12-14; 143, 10; Is. 4, 4; 11, 2-3; 32, 15-17; Ezek. 11, 19-20; 36, 25-27; 37, 14; Zech. 12, 10).

Throughout the course of these various functions, the Spirit tends to designate a permanent divine influence while the Word tends to be attributed to limited or transitory interventions. Thus it abides with certain prophetic (Num. 11, 17-25; 2 Kgs. 2, 9. 15), royal (1 Sam. 16, 13) and messianic (Is. 11, 42, 1; 61, 1) personages, and in retrospective overviews of the past it appears as the constant guide of the chosen people (Is. 63, 10-11. 14; Neh. 9, 20), with whom it remains present (Hg. 2, 5). Finally, while Ezekiel sees it acting on a transcendent plane to ensure the presence of Yahweh in various places (1, 12-20), the book of Wisdom makes it a supracosmic energy that "fills the universe, is all-embracing, and knows man's utterance" (Wis. 1, 7).

## Wisdom

In the book of Wisdom we also find an original approach that represents the culmination of a long evolution in sapiential literature. The Spirit and the Word are fused with Wisdom. I shall not trace the evolution of this approach, but it would be helpful to note the two poles of biblical speculation on divine Wisdom.

One pole stresses the transcendent nature of Wisdom. It is prior to creation (Prv. 8, 22ff.; Sir. 1, 4). It inspired the creator (Jb. 28, 25-27; Sir. 1, 19; Wis. 8, 4), serving as his instrument (Prv. 3, 19; Jer. 10, 12) and collaborator (Prv. 8, 30; Wis. 7, 12. 21; 8, 6; 14, 5). It knows the universe in depth: its mysterious design, its laws, and the *raison d'être* of everything. Such knowledge remains inaccessible to man (Jb. 28, 1-23; Bar. 3, 15-31), who must remain within the limits of his own peculiar condition (Jb. 28, 28; Sir. 3, 21-24; see also Gn. 3, 5. 22; Ezek. 28, 1-5). As the attribute of him who alone deserves to be called wise (Jb. 12, 13; Sir. 1, 8), and the personification of his counsel (cf. Is. 40, 2; Wis. 8, 13-14) or his providential government (Prv. 8, 15-16; Jb. 12, 13-25), Wisdom defies human foresight and sagacity (cf. Jb. 11, 6).

At the other pole, Wisdom sometimes appears as the friend of man. It has been with man from the beginning (Prv. 8, 31), and it invites him in countless ways to choose the paths of justice and stay on them (Prv. 1, 20ff.; 8, 1-11. 32-36; 9, 1-6). Essentially it teaches him to live in "fear of the Lord" (Prv. 1, 7; Jb. 28, 28; etc.). But it also teaches him volumes of wisdom about life—a fund of knowledge that is spread about among many nations and that was especially embodied in Solomon (1 Kgs. 5, 9-14). It is also depicted as a saving force. It guided the first steps of men, and it intervened in primitive history to deliver them and save them (Wis. 10, 1-8). It protected the nation's ancestors (Wis. 10, 9-14) and fostered its growth (Wis. 10, 15—11, 1). It is also identified with the privileged revelation dispensed to Israel, which culminates in the law (Dt. 4, 5-8; Sir. 24, 23; Bar. 3, 37—4, 4). Finally, it incarnates or symbolizes the presence of grace and God's favor. For although it rules the whole universe, it chose to dwell with Israel; in particular, it resides in the temple of Jerusalem, where it presides over cultic worship (Sir. 24, 6-12).

This narrowing of its field of action is only apparent and temporary. The Bible underlines its activity throughout the whole cosmos. It rules the world with power, governing it as a providential force (Wis. 7, 24; 8, 1). It prefers to remain with man, whom it loves (Wis. 1, 6). It can give man every possible kind of knowledge (Wis. 7, 17-21; 8, 8), but it is primarily concerned with forming him in virtue and piety (Wis. 1, 4-5; 8, 7; 10, 12). In the course of time, it passes into holy souls, producing "friends of God and prophets" (Wis. 7, 27). This holy influence is a privileged aspect of its active presence in the world.

At the same time Wisdom is identified as closely as possible with God, being the immediate radiation of his transcendence (Wis. 7, 25-26). We cannot compare it to an intermediary reality in the strict sense, for instead it personifies God's activity itself in its source and its effects. It is an activity wholly impregnated with God's primary attributes, which are both transcendent and immanent and which effectively guide individual and collective history toward its true end. Through the complex of biblical traits associated with it, Wisdom presages a special gift of God, his permanent habitation among men, and the unification of all his plans in a reality that is both divine and very close to man.

John Crossan/*Chicago, Illinois*

# The Presence of God's Love in the Power of Jesus' Works

T he meeting of God and man in Jesus Christ will be considered in only one aspect here. Factors such as the union in Jesus of the divine Word incarnated in a human nature, the understanding which Jesus himself had of his own being and his own mission, and the distinction between what he had himself declared during his life and what the Spirit had assisted the disciples to comprehend after his death and resurrection present problems too numerous and complex to be treated in such a short article.

## I

### STATEMENT OF THE PROBLEM

It suffices to recall here the main lines of the general problem [1] before turning to the particular aspect to be considered in

---

[1] On this subject, cf. O. Betz, "The Christological Problem in New Testament Research of Today," in *Encounter* 27 (1964), pp. 54-64; R. Brown, "How Much Did Jesus Know?—A Survey of the Biblical Evidence," in *Cath. Bib. Quart.* 29 (1967), pp. 315-45; C. Ceroke, "The Divinity of Christ in the Gospels," in *Cath. Bib. Quart.* 24 (1962), pp. 125-39; L. Malavez, "Jésus de l'histoire, fondement de la foi," in *Nouv. Rev. Théol.* 89 (1967), pp. 785-99; C. O'Collins, "Revelation as History," in *Heyth. Journ.* 7 (1966), pp. 394-406; B. Vawter, "History and the Word," in *Cath. Bib. Quart.* 29 (1967), pp. 512-23.

detail. This problem touches on two profoundly controverted areas, neither of which is anywhere near solution or even consensus. The entire problem of the historical Jesus is still an open discussion. What did Jesus do and say in his own life and his own time and his own place as distinct from what the primitive communities in their own oral traditions and evangelical confessions recall and record of him for their differing catechetical, liturgical and polemical necessities? Within this general problematic, or maybe even at its core, is a second difficulty. This concerns the self-consciousness of the historical Jesus. How did Jesus actually see himself and understand his own identity? We need not reject our own modern theories concerning crises in identity or our own sometimes masochistic penchant for introspection into this Jesus in order to establish a valid and meaningful question with regard to his understanding of himself. The questions which are asked so repeatedly in, for example, the gospel of Mark must have had some earlier and more interior analogues in questions asked about Jesus for himself and to himself.

These questions would have arisen in some continuity with the religious tradition of which Jesus was the recipient. One basic characteristic of this heritage was its preference for discussions and analyses concerning the divine will and the divine intention. The God of this tradition was understood not so much from metaphysical investigations into being as from confessional investigations into history. In the same way, the Israelites received their clearest self-understanding about their destiny as God's covenanted people from their ongoing history in whose weal and woe were seen the salvation and the judgment of this God's grand design. It is to be expected that Jesus' awareness of his own identity and his comprehension of his own mission would have arisen not so much from some philosophical idea, but from meditation on the meaning of history, and most proximately and precisely on the meaning of his own personal history and on the analysis of events in his own most concrete experience. The titles Jesus uses or accepts for himself and the

traditional categories from the Old Testament or the intertesta-
mental literature that are placed on his own or his audience's
lips may or may not stem from the actualities of his life situation.
Scholarship has still far to go in discussing such terms as Lord,
Messiah, Servant of God, Son of Man, the Logos, and many
others. But if one by one such categories of identification are
attributed rather to the early Church's confession of Jesus than
to Jesus' comprehension of himself, the question is inevitably
pressed: How did Jesus understand his own mission and his
own destiny?

## II

### THE JESUS OF POWER

In summing up anyone's life, be it in historical or confessional language, the categories of words and deeds or teachings
and activities are a fairly obvious differentiation.[2] The people
in the synagogue at Capernaum distinguished Jesus' teaching and
Jesus' authority or power of exorcism in this way: "Here is a
teaching that is new . . . and with authority behind it: he gives
orders even to unclean spirits and they obey him" (Mk. 1,
27). In a similar distinction, those in the synagogue at
Nazareth wondered: "Where did the man get all this? What is
this wisdom that has been granted him, and these miracles that
are worked through him?" (Mk. 6, 2). The entire first volume
of his own work is summarized in these same categories by Luke.
In Acts 1, 1 he recalls how his "earlier work . . . dealt with
everything Jesus had done and taught". This section will focus
on what Jesus did, on his miracles and his power, in order to

[2] On this subject, cf. H. Baltensweiler, "Wunder und Glaube im Neuen
Testament," in *Theol. Zeit.* 23 (1967), pp. 241-56; E. Gutwenger, "Die
Machterweise Jesu formgeschichtlicher Sicht," in *Zeit. Kath. Theol.* 89
(1967), pp. 176-90; K. Kertelge, "Zur Interpretation der Wunder Jesu.
Ein Literaturbericht," in *Bib. Leb.* 9 (1968), pp. 140-53; J. McKenzie,
"Signs and Power. The New Testament Presentation of Miracles," in
*Chicago Studies* 3 (1964), pp. 5-18.

attempt to gain access to his own initial understanding of his mission.

## The Meaning of "Miracle"

The term "miracle" must be understood in its biblical sense and not in the modern concept, whether that modern understanding be from the side of traditional Christian belief or classical rationalistic disbelief in its actuality. In the biblical mentality Yahweh is Lord of all creation and of all history, and as such he is the cause of all natural phenomena and all historical events. Yahweh is not the periodic interventionist who changes the closed sequence of "natural" events through some special "supernatural" interruption. Since Yahweh is in total control of life, the only valid distinction is between his more important or significant actions and the less striking or more ordinary activities attributed to his power. In this tradition one would not confess God's supernatural intervention over against the laws of nature but would rather speak of God's "greatness and . . . power . . . whose works and mighty deeds no one in heaven or on earth can rival" (Dt. 3, 24). All such actions tell something about the being of God, and the greater the work he has performed, the more profound the intuition into his being and, more importantly, into his plans and his designs. Miracles are not so much proofs that God exists as signs and indications of who God is and what God wants.

## The Miracle as Power

This same mentality underlies the New Testament thinking on Jesus' miracles and is reflected necessarily in the vocabulary used to describe his actions. The term *thaymasia,* "wonders or wonderful things", is used in Matthew 21, 14-15: "There were also blind and lame people who came to him in the temple, and he cured them. At the sight of these wonderful things. . . ." The word *semeion* is used exclusively by John for such actions of Jesus which signify and reveal another world hidden behind them.

Apart from this special usage in the Johannine theology, the Synoptics have the expression in one of the controversies with the Pharisees: "The Pharisees came up and started a discussion with him; they demanded of him a sign from heaven, to test him" (cf. Mk. 8, 11 and parallels). The same term appears in similar circumstances when "Herod was delighted to see Jesus; he had heard about him and had been wanting for a long time to set eyes on him; moreover, he was hoping to see some miracle (*semeion*) *worked by him*" (Lk. 23, 8).

However, in the general Synoptic tradition the more ordinary and more frequent term for Jesus' miracles is *dynameis*, "powers or mighty deeds", and it is in this sense that the expression "the Jesus of power" is used in this section. The word is used in the plural when Herod discusses Jesus as the resurrected Baptist and explains his "miraculous powers" through this hypothesis (Mt. 14, 2; Mk. 6, 14). The inhabitants of Nazareth likewise discuss his "miraculous powers" and his "miracles" (Mt. 13, 54. 58; Mk. 6, 2. 5). The plural *dynameis* is placed on Jesus' own lips in castigating the disbelief which greeted his "miracles" in the towns of Chorazin, Bethsaida, and Capernaum (Mt. 11, 20-23; Lk. 10, 13-15). The singular term, *dynamis,* appears in the cure of the woman with a hemorrhage as Jesus, having been touched, is "immediately aware that power had gone out from him" (Mk. 5, 30; Lk. 8, 46). So also "everyone in the crowd was trying to touch him because power came out of him that cured them all" (Lk. 6, 19). Once—in Luke 5, 17—this power is attributed directly to God: "And the power of the Lord was behind his works of healing."

Besides being used for Jesus' miracles, the word is also used for the miraculous powers which Jesus gives to his own disciples. The followers of Jesus "work many miracles in his name" (Mt. 7, 22). Jesus talks of "one who works a miracle in my name" (Mk. 9, 39) and promises: "I have given you power to tread underfoot serpents and scorpions" (Lk. 10, 19). From all of this it is clear that, from the most ordinary term used for Jesus' miracles, they are seen as powers and as signs and manifestations of God's own power operative in and through Jesus. This view is summed up in Acts 2, 22: "Jesus the Nazarene was a man commended to you by God by the miracles (*dynamesi*) and portents (*terasi*) and signs (*semeiois*) that God worked through him when he was among you."

It is on these powers of Jesus that this article will concentrate. This is not to argue that the teachings of Jesus, be they ethical or apocalyptic, or the titles of Jesus, be they novel or traditional, can tell us nothing about the historical Jesus but reveal only the reactions of the primitive communities to that Jesus reseen as the risen Christ. The scholarly debate on this must still be considered as being quite far from final resolution. Neither does it contend that the narrations of Jesus' miraculous powers have not been heavily edited and profoundly affected in the evangelical records. Indeed many of the processes of readaptation can be as clearly seen in the retelling of what Jesus did as they can be found in the retelling of what Jesus said. Miracles can be recast just as easily as teachings, and both are equally open to being invented to fulfill some communal necessity. For example, the elimination of the disedifying is already at work on the two miracles in Mark 7, 31-37 and 8, 21-26. In each case Jesus uses spittle (*ptysas*), to touch the tongue of the dumb man in the Decapolis (7, 33) and the eyes of the blind man of Bethsaida (8, 23). This realism and the apparent difficulty of the cure in 8, 25 ("Then he laid his hands on the man's eyes again") caused both Matthew and Luke to omit both these cures from their own accounts.

Or again, the process of the symbolization of the historical can be seen in the miracle of Mark 5, 25-34 and Luke 8, 43-48 when compared with Matthew 9, 20-22. In the former two accounts the woman's illness is immediately cured when she touches Jesus (Mk. 5, 29; Lk. 8, 44). But in Matthew there is no such immediate cure. It is the Word of Jesus and not the cloak of Jesus that cures her in Matthew 9, 22: "Jesus . . . said to her, 'Courage, my daughter, your faith has restored you to health.' And from that moment the woman was well again." The point of the change is obvious: the Word of Jesus is still available for the believer even if the cloak is gone forever. Hence the reason for choosing Jesus' miraculous activities as the point of entry into his self-consciousness is not because they have not been subject to less change and development than other areas of his life. The reason is rather that it is only in the area of his power that there are still extant indications of self-questioning and of the conflict and tension out of which self-identity and self-awareness are finally and irrevocably forged. This will be indicated in greater detail in the next major section of this article.

## III

### THE TEMPTATION OF POWER

Whatever growth and development there was within the doctrinal thought of Jesus is extremely difficult if not forever impossible to discover in the present Gospel records.[3] Such can be found, analyzed and demonstrated within the oral traditions and written records in which the early communities recalled his teachings, but these show the changes in the Church's usage and understanding rather than changes in the thought of Jesus himself. In the case of his miraculous powers, his *dynameis,* there are, however, certain episodes which help to indicate his own attitude toward himself, his mission and the function of his power. These are the three temptations narrated in detail in Matthew 4, 1-11 and Luke 4, 1-13 and mentioned in passing summary in Mark 1, 13.

[3] On this subject, cf. J. Dupont, "L'origine du récit des tentations de Jésus au désert," in *Rev. Bib.* 73 (1966), pp. 30-76; N. Hyldahl, "Die Versuchung auf der Zinne des Tempels (Matth 4, 5-7 = Luk 4, 9-12)," in *Stud. Theol.* 15 (1961), pp. 113-27; H. Kee, "The Terminology of Mark's Exorcism Stories," in *New Test. Stud.* 14 (1968), pp. 232-46; H. Kelly, "The Devil in the Desert," in *Cath. Bib. Quart.* 26 (1964), pp. 190-220.

## The Source of the Narratives

The immediate and most obvious problem is whether the temptation narratives stem from Jesus himself or represent catechetical creations of the early communities. It is clear that the temptation stories have received redactional changes in their final evangelical recasting. The sequence goes from the desert to the temple to the mountain in Matthew 4, 2-4. 5-7. 8-10, but from the desert to the mountain to the temple in Luke 4, 3-4. 5-8. 9-12. Luke has climaxed his infancy narration by two episodes concerning Jesus' presence in the temple in 2, 22-40 and 2, 41-52. In line with this overture the public life of Jesus likewise reaches its climax in a carefully chronicled journey southward toward Jerusalem and its temple in 9, 51. 53. 57; 10, 1. 38; 13, 22. 33; 17, 11; 18, 31. 35; 19, 1. 11. 28. 41-44. Finally he reaches the temple in 19, 47, and at the end the last word of the Gospel is that the disciples, awaiting the Spirit's advent, "were continually in the temple praising God" (24, 53). Given the three temptations, it is obvious why Luke would place the temple trial in last place even though the natural climax of content would place the mountain event in the final position, as in Matthew.

It can also be argued that many of the motifs found in the narrations reflect the voice of the early Church rather than the voice of the historical Jesus. The twice repeated "if you are the Son of God" in Matthew 4, 3. 6 is not repeated in the third and final test in 4, 9 as if to suggest that Satan by then knows that he is the Messiah, the Son of God. And the rebuttal of the temptations by the three quotations from Deuteronomy 8, 3; 6, 16, and 6, 13 in Matthew 4, 4. 7. 10 and Luke 4, 4. 12. 8 respectively shows Jesus as the true Israel negating by his fidelity in the desert Israel's ancient failure in a similar situation.

But when all this is acknowledged as pertaining to reinterpretation and readaptation for the confessional and catechetical needs of the community, there is still left the *fact* of the confrontation between Jesus and Satan and the *three* encounters—

in the desert, in the temple, and on the mountain—in which it is summarized. The contention here is that this hard core stems from Jesus himself and not from the early Church.

There are two basic arguments for this, one negative and one positive. It is very difficult to imagine the early Church creating a conflict between Jesus and Satan in which, even though eventually unsuccessful, Satan acts on Jesus with rather free and sovereign power and in which Jesus' reactions are no more than those which might be expected from any devout Israelite. Second, and more positively, the triple format and the climax of the temptation narratives are characteristic features of Jesus' own creative teaching, especially in the parables.[4] Examples of this are: the three losses and the three gains of the sower parable (Mk. 4, 3-8); the three servants sent to the wicked overseers (Lk. 20, 9-18); the three measures (Lk. 13, 20); the three excuses of those invited to the great banquet (Lk. 14, 16-24); the three amounts left with the servants by the departing master (Mt. 25, 14-30); the three reactions to the wounded man on the road between Jerusalem and Jericho (Lk. 10, 29-37). For these two basic reasons it is argued that the *fact* of the confrontation and the *triple* format of its narration derive from the teaching of Jesus and not from the catechetical creativity of the early Church.

## The Contents of the Temptations

By the content of the temptations is meant their function as Jesus told them, rather than their present fuller content as used by the community in the different redactions of Matthew and Luke.

The core of the temptation is not for Jesus to doubt his power but for Jesus to abuse his power. It is this possibility of abuse which links all three of them together. The order preserved in Matthew will be followed here: in the desert, on the pinnacle of the temple, and atop the mountain.

The first two trials concern rather specific betrayals of his

---

[4] Cf. C. Mitton, "Threefoldness in the Teaching of Jesus," in *Exp. Times* 75 (1964), pp. 228-30; P. Ackroyd, *ibid.*, p. 316.

miraculous power, while the third and final one is more general and includes all such possibilities. In the first trial Jesus is tempted to use his power merely for his own personal convenience: to alleviate perfectly normal—and indeed meritorious—hunger by turning stones into bread. This test would represent an abuse of his power with regard to himself. The second trial would be an abuse of power with regard to others. The location of the temptation is very important. To descend from the parapet of the temple would ensure the maximum audience and publicity for the feat. The temptation is to use his power to convince others, to elicit by his power cheap awe and call it faith. The third and climactic temptation is not so much another specific possibility of abuse but the category under which all such abuse would fall. It is to obtain the full accomplishment of power by placing it at Satan's command. Each and every abuse of Jesus' power would remove that gift from the realm of God and bow down before Satan by entering his kingdom. To abuse his power either with regard to himself (first temptation) or to others (second temptation) would be to join the realm of Satan (third temptation).

Most interesting, however, is the fact that there is no temptation for Jesus to doubt his power; there is only the possibility of its wrong use. To this extent and only to this extent are we allowed to see the conflict within Jesus' own self-awareness. He knows that his power is an awesome responsibility and that it can be abused, and he even specifies two precise ways in which such abuse could take place. But it is not possible to get back before the moment when the presence of that power was known. We begin with its presence accepted and only its abuse as problematic.

## The Function of Jesus' Power

The three temptations are negative reflections which help us to see the function which Jesus attributed to the gift of power he had received. Following the leads of these archetypal temptations, we can notice patterns of what Jesus *does not do* with his miraculous powers during the public ministry. As in the first temptation, he does not use them for his own ease or convenience or even for his own defense and protection, and even less to attack others who endanger him. This is still reflected in the evangelical retelling of the arrest in Gethsemane in Matthew 26, 53: "Do you think that I cannot appeal to my Father who would promptly send more than twelve legions of angels to my defense?'

Following the lead of the second trial, Jesus steadily refuses to use his miracles to prove himself or his mission when confronted with accusation or disbelief. This is true despite all classical apologetics can do to use the miracles as proofs of identity and vindication of function. Proofs would have been useful for the opposition of the Pharisees, and yet their request for "a sign from heaven", a miracle akin to the temptation of descending before the startled crowd from the pinnacle of the temple, is categorically refused (cf. Mk. 8, 11-13 and parallels). Proofs would also be useful for pagans, and yet the two very explicit miracles for Gentiles take place after quite staggering acts of faith. The centurion of Capernaum receives the cure of his servant after a confession of faith in Jesus' power that elicits the reply: "Nowhere in Israel have I found faith like this" (Mt. 8, 5-13), and the pagan Syrophoenician argued back to Jesus that she had the right to the crumbs beneath Israel's table (Mk. 7, 24-30). Jesus does not use his power to create faith or to force into faith those who do not wish to believe.

Finally, the third temptation is dramatically recalled in the accusation of Satanic collusion (cf. Mk. 3, 22-30 and parallels). This is the only ultimate refuge from the fact of Jesus' power—it is enacted under Satan's dominion. And Jesus' iron reply is the only answer. If the power is used to fight the realm of evil, how can it belong to the kingdom of evil? Or do you wish to state that the driving out of a demoniac is not a good act but an evil act?

These negatives all serve to highlight the positive function of Jesus' power. All his miraculous power is unleashed in response to human need: sight to the blind, hearing to the deaf, speech

to the dumb, strength to the lame, health to the leprous, freedom
to the possessed, wisdom to the ignorant, forgiveness to the sinful.
No matter how much prophetic fulfillment is read back into
these miracles in their present retelling, it is still this quality of
mercy and kindness that most clearly shines through them all.
No matter how much of the liturgical theory or the catechetical
practice of the early Church has changed their final content, it is
still this response of love and compassion that holds them all
most deeply together. No matter how much the apologetical or
polemical purposes of the individual evangelist has molded their
present shape, it is still this aspect of help and assistance that
clarifies most exactly their function in the mind of Jesus.

## IV

### THE KINGDOM OF POWER

This analysis of the function of Jesus' miracles as full
response to human need is confirmed in Jesus' own teaching.
The theme of the kingdom and the use of parables are as
characteristic of his pedagogy and as basic to his thought as the
use of miraculous healing is to his activity. The illustration of the
rule and the realm of God in terms of everyday imagery is but
another manifestation of Jesus' attempt to respond to human
need—in this case, to instruct the ignorant in concepts and categories they were most likely to comprehend. Because of the
critical difficulties in separating Jesus' teachings from those
placed on his lips by the early Church, we can limit consideration
here to two key parables, that of the last judgment in Matthew
25, 31-46 and that of the good Samaritan in Luke 10, 29-37.
Each one is sufficiently basic to Jesus' thought to be used
independently as an example of how he understood his own
power and its usage.[5]

[5] On this subject, cf. G. Castellino, "Il Sacerdote e il Levita nella
parabola del buon samaritano," in *Divinitas* 9 (1965), pp. 134-40; G.
Lampe, "Secularization in the New Testament and the Early Church,"
in *Theology* 71 (1968), pp. 163-75; J. Michaels, "Apostolic Hardships

## The Parables of Concern

In the parable of the final judgment the just are those who have responded to human need, summed up in six categories of pain: hunger, thirst, loneliness, cold, sickness and imprisonment. The just are those who have responded affirmatively to these varying types of human anguish. Then it is the turn of the unjust. It might be expected that these would be the ones who robbed the bread of the hungry man, or took his water, or stole his clothes, or destroyed the house of the poor, or beat or imprisoned unjustly those who were defenseless. It might be expected that the unjust would be those who had done wrong, but actually they are those who have done nothing. They are those who, confronted with the same six categories of human anguish, did nothing to alleviate their presence. The division into just and unjust is not so much a split between those who love and those who hate as between those who respond to human need and those who do not so respond. Those who do positive evil are not even considered or discussed. The just and the unjust are the concerned and the unconcerned. That, says Jesus, is how judgment will be made.

The same division between those who respond to human anguish and those who do nothing, together with this same ignoring of those who do positive evil, is found in the parable of the good Samaritan. Once again the point is basic: "What must I do to inherit eternal life?" (Lk. 10, 25). The brigands who "took all he had, beat him and then made off, leaving him half dead" are clear representatives of positive evil. But in the final analysis Jesus ignores them and concentrates on the priest and the Levite who "passed by on the other side" when they saw the man lying on the road, as contrasted with the Samaritan whose actions are a precise and exact response to all the man's needs for medication, transportation, shelter and convalescence.

and Righteous Gentiles. A Study of Mt. 25, 31-46," in *Journ. Bib. Lit.* 84 (1965), pp. 27-37; W. Pannenberg, "The Kingdom of God and the Foundation of Ethics," in *Una Sancta* 25 (1968), pp. 6-26.

The final question is: "Which of these three, do you think, proved himself a neighbor to the man?" (Lk. 10, 36). Once again the division is between the Samaritan who responded to human need and the proponents of formal religion who did nothing for him. The brigands are ignored, for they were already fully judged by the ten commandments. But Jesus' teaching is that the opposite of love is not only hate but also unconcern, that the opposite of a good response is not only an evil response but also the lack of any response at all.

Thus, there is complete harmony between the basic activity of Jesus' miraculous powers and the basic teaching of such key parables as these. Jesus understands his power as operative only in response to human need, and he teaches that such response is what makes a man just in God's sight and that the corresponding injustice is that of the man who does nothing in the face of human anguish.

### The Threat of Jesus

From all of this it is clear that the summary of Jesus' life in Acts 10, 38-39 leaves out one very important facet of his ministry. This omission leaves the opposition and the crucifixion inexplicable. "God had anointed him with the Holy Spirit and with power (*dynamei*), and because God was with him, Jesus went about doing good and curing all who had fallen into the power of the devil. Now I, and those with me, can witness to everything he did . . . and also to the fact that they killed him by hanging him on a tree. . . .' But Jesus did much more than do good and cure. He stated that such acts of power as response to human need represented the arrival of the realm and rule of God. From this principle it followed logically, and was even stated explicitly by Jesus, that God was not primarily interested in a quiet sabbath or a full temple or a washed cup, but that God, the God of Jesus, was primarily interested in all that healed man's ancient anguish, and that the community of those who so acted represented the just on whom his rule had descended and who formed together his realm. To respond to the spectrum of human need would hardly breed opposition from anyone, let alone crucifixion. To state that this is the kingdom of God, the will of the Father, and the heart of religion, to which all else can be but the means to the end or the signs to the reality, could and did cost a man his life.

The meeting of God and man in Jesus is the meeting between the God of total power and the man of total concern. It announces a kingdom in which the power to heal human anguish and liberate mankind toward his future stems in all its ways from God but can operate only through human love, described rather than defined as response to the individual's present pain from the one who there confronts him. In Jesus it was not a suggested idea but a lived life, and it began with the need to understand and explain the gift of God and the power of healing which he found within himself.

Ulrich Luz/*Mannedorf, Switzerland*

# New Testament Perspectives of the Image of God in Christ and Mankind

The likeness of God in man is an interesting question for Protestant-Catholic theological discussion. According to the Catholic view, which finds its classic formulation in the work of Peter Lombard,[1] a distinction must be made between the *imago Dei* ("image of God") and the *similitudo Dei* ("likeness of God") in man; the former is part of the perduring essence of man, while the latter is the state of original justice that can easily be lost. According to the reformationist viewpoint, man's likeness to God was essentially lost in Adam's fall; therefore we cannot distinguish between intact human nature and the *donum superaditum* of original justice.[2] However, reformationist theology did not carry this thesis through to its ultimate conclusions, but left the whole matter suspended in mid-air.

The conceptual distinction between *similitudo* and *imago* rests upon an erroneous exegesis of the parallel terms in Genesis 1, 26f. In the Old Testament the two terms are synonymous, and no distinction is made between them in the New Testament either. The ordinary term in the New Testament is *eikon*

---

[1] Petrus Lombardus, *Sent.* II, 16, 3.
[2] Material can be found in O. Weber, *Grundlagen der Dogmatik* I (Neukirchen, [2]1959), p. 625, footnotes 1 and 2.

("image"). The New Testament, however, does allow us to probe more deeply into this matter if we start out by asking two basic questions: (1) To what extent does the New Testament refer to mankind in general as the image of God? (2) To what extent does it apply this designation solely to men who have been re-created in Christ?

The first noteworthy fact is that remarks about Christ being God's *eikon* are found almost exclusively in the Pauline corpus. They are absent in the gospels, even where we find closely related expressions (e.g., in Mt. 25, 31ff.). Moreover, most of Paul's statements about the *eikon* are traditional, deriving from the Judaeo-Hellenistic communities that predated or were contemporary with Paul. We shall go into detail as we proceed, but it is worth noting that the pre-Pauline communities represent a central focal point.[3]

# I

## NATURAL MAN AS THE LIKENESS OF GOD

There is really no talk about this in the New Testament. The most important Pauline text is 1 Corinthians 11, 7 where Paul seeks to provide a basis for the Jewish tradition that women must wear a veil in church. Alluding to Genesis 1, 27 and expressing agreement with certain rabbis,[4] Paul asserts that the man (and only he!) is the image of God. Because of her lower place, the woman should wear a covering on her head.

Here Paul is probably basing his remarks directly on the rabbinical exegesis of Genesis 1, 26f. In verse 3 of this chapter, he sets up a triad (God-Christ-man) similar to the one in 1 Corinthians 3, 22f. But in verse 7, it turns out that Christ is left out of the series. We can more readily understand why he

---

[3] Among the most important recent works are: F. Eltester, *Eikon im Neuen Testament* (Berlin, 1958); J. Jervell, *Imago Dei* (Göttingen, 1960); E. Larsson, *Christus als Vorbild* (Uppsale, 1962).

[4] See Jervell, *op. cit.,* pp. 109ff.

does this if we realize that his talk about Christ as the image of God is often related to talk about the transformation of the old man and the elimination of the once existing differences between creatures (see Col. 3, 11 and Gal. 3, 28). In 1 Corinthians 11, 7 Paul deliberately avoids this line of thought. So here we have a singular statement by Paul which seems to be taken over from Jewish tradition, and which cannot readily be harmonized with the rest of his statements on this subject.

James 3, 9 is the second relevant text here. It is wholly in line with the Jewish tradition of exhortatory admonitions.[5] Typically Jewish is the admonition about the evil potential of the tongue which can praise God and curse men made in his likeness. Also typically Jewish is the appeal to the likeness of God in man in order to put more bite into the exhortation. It is our neighbor's likeness to God that gives him his dignity and makes our contempt of him a sin against God. As in 1 Corinthians 11, 7, there is no indication as to what constitutes man's likeness to God.

These are the only places in the New Testament where natural man as such is presented as the image of God. It is peculiar and striking that this doctrine plays such a small role in the New Testament. It is also noteworthy that in both texts the theme crops up in an exhortatory context where the Jewish background is evident. We definitely cannot say that the Christian faith reworked this Jewish theme, nor that the New Testament provides us with focal texts on natural man's likeness to God.

The situation is quite different when we look for texts that talk about Christ and the new man as the image of God. In the pre-Pauline community especially, we can see a real *eikon* theology.

[5] The pertinent material is summarized best in F. Mussner, *Der Jakobusbrief* (Freiburg-Basel-Vienna, 1964), pp. 167f.

## II
### THE EIKON THEOLOGY OF THE PRE-PAULINE COMMUNITIES

### Christ as God's Eikon

The most important text is Colossians 1, 15. Christ is "the image (*eikon*) of the invisible God, the first-born of all creation". The phrase is part of a hymn which the author of this epistle [6] included here. There is general agreement that it was a Christian hymn of two strophes dedicated to Christ.[7] The first strophe praised Christ as the mediator of creation, while the second strophe praised him as the redeemer. Even the first strophe was sung from the standpoint of those redeemed by Christ, for only the redeemed know that Christ had a hand in creation, and only they realize that creation as a whole has been gathered into indissoluble unity by Christ. Baptism was apparently the occasion on which this hymn was used by the community. E. Käsemann has made a good case that verses 13 and 14 of Colossians 1, which lead up to our text, derive from a baptismal liturgy.[8] Re-created and reborn by baptism, the faithful praise Christ as creator and redeemer.

What does the text mean when it says that Christ is the *eikon* of the invisible God? It does not seem to be a direct interpretation of Genesis 1, 26ff.; the attempts to explain the hymn of Colossians as an interpretation of Genesis 1 must be regarded as failures.[9] The case here seems to be similar to that of John's

[6] I maintain that Colossians and Ephesians were not written by Paul himself but rather by one of his disciples.

[7] For a summary see the report of H. Gabathuler, *Jesus Christus: Haupt der Kirche, Haupt der Welt* (Zurich, 1965) pp. 125ff. The most recent interpretations of the text are to be found in E. Schweitzer and R. Schnackenburg, "Kolossser 1, 15-20," in *Evangelisch-katholischer Kommentar zum N.T.: Vorarbeiten I* (Einsiedeln = Neukirchen, 1969), pp. 7ff. and 33ff.

[8] E. Käsemann, "Eine urchristliche Taufliturgie," in *Exegetische Versuche und Besinnungen* I (Göttingen, 1960) pp. 34-51, esp. pp. 43ff.

[9] See especially those cited by E. Lohse, *Die Briefe an die Kolosser und an Philemon* (Göttingen, 1968), p. 85.

prologue and the hymn in Philippians (2, 6-11). Serving as the backdrop for the hymn are certain Judaeo-Hellenistic notions about a mediator of creation: the divine Logos or divine Wisdom. Philo, for example, applies the term, God's *eikon*, to the Logos, to Wisdom, and to the first, spiritual man.[10] To say that Christ is the *eikon* of God does not mean that he is the embodiment or true face of the humanity which God created in Genesis 1; it means that Christ, in an exclusive sense, is the one who reveals God to the world.

A further point is relevant here. In speaking of Christ as the *eikon* of God, the text is not speaking of the earthly Jesus. The term applies only to the risen Christ. The historical Jesus, *qua* man, is not the image of God; it is the risen and pre-existent Christ who rules the whole cosmos that is the *eikon* of God. This may explain why it was difficult, if not impossible, for Christians to see natural, unresurrected mankind as the image of God.

If the *risen* Christ is the image of God, then natural man could not be the image of God by his very nature. For Christ, as the *eikon* of God, is not part of the world; he stands as God's representative over against the world. Even though everything was created by him and through him, the hymn of Colossians stresses that he himself is *before* all and the *head* of the body (which probably means "the world" in the hymn itself).

To speak of Christ as God's *eikon* is to say something about his very nature—namely that he is not a worldly but a divine being. In singing this hymn, the Christian community was professing that God was accessible to them *only* in his *eikon*, Jesus Christ. Jesus Christ is not only an aspect of God; he is the visible *essence* of the invisible God. God is accessible only in his *eikon*.

The community which sang this hymn had little interest in the earthly Jesus and his life, even as it gave little thought to the reality of worldly suffering. It also had little interest in

[10] See Eltester, *op. cit.,* pp. 34ff.

the distinction between salvation already accomplished and salvation yet to come. Instead the hymn focuses on the work of creation and redemption already accomplished, and it allows everything, even the future, to be subsumed under this head. To be sure, Colossians 1, 15-20 does not rule out God's salvific activity in the future, but it subsumes this future under the reality of already accomplished redemption.

To this extent, Colossians 1, 15-20 is quite comparable to Philippians 2, 6-11. Both hymns come from pre-Pauline communities that tend to base their life on the present reality of salvation. We shall dub communities with this tendency as "enthusiastic"; it is in them that we find the *eikon* motif which bespeaks the here-and-now presence and knowability of God in Jesus Christ.

Another important text is 2 Corinthians 4, 4. Here, too, Paul is deeply dependent on formulations that stem from the community. The contrast between "those saved" and "those perishing" likely stems from the community at Corinth,[11] as does the phrase "the God of this world";[12] the notion of predestination is also at home in the pre-Pauline "enthusiastic" communities.[13] Considering Colossians 1, 15ff., it seems that the phrase "who is the image of God" also fits into this milieu. To be sure, we should not assume that Paul is citing a finished, ready-made formula; instead he is entering into debate with his opponents, adopting their idiom and motifs from 2 Corinthians 3, 4-18 which are deeply impregnated with traditional notions.

What is the import of Paul's *eikon* teaching here? It primarily deals with knowledge of God. Along with *eikon* we find the notion of "glory" which, on the basis of 2 Corinthians 3, 18, must be regarded as its synonym. Paul is talking about

[11] See U. Luz, *Das Geschichtsverständnis des Paulus* (Munich, 1968), pp. 255f.

[12] There is no other similar formulation in Paul's works; the closest parallels are in John (e.g., 12, 31; 14, 30; 16, 11), which also derive from an "enthusiastic" community environment.

[13] See Luz, *op. cit.*, pp. 252, 256, 258, 260ff.

the proclamation of the Gospel by Jesus Christ and the knowledge of God's glory. Christ is the *eikon* of God insofar as he makes knowledge of God possible. He is the nature of God insofar as it is visible and recognizable. God is represented in the *eikon*.

On the basis of 2 Corinthians 3, 18 we could say this: The *eikon* of God is God's glory insofar as it shines on our faces— that is, insofar as it is turned toward us. It is also evident here that *eikon* applies to the risen Christ, to the Lord (v. 5) who enlightens the hearts of the faithful in the proclamation of the Word. One difference between this text and Colossians 1, 15 is that here the cosmological aspect of the *eikon* motif fades into the background.

If we look for further data in the New Testament, we find texts where typical motifs of *eikon* christology are present without the word *eikon* itself being used. Closely related to Colossians 1, 15ff. is Hebrews 1, 2f. Here, too, we read about the one who cooperated in creation and sustains it. Here, too, the resurrection and glorification of Christ play a central role (as in Col. 1, 18ff.). But here Christ is not called the *eikon* of God; he is called the "reflection" and "stamp" of God's glory.

Both concepts, like *eikon*, derive from Jewish speculation on wisdom (*sophia*). Their meaning is the same: "reflection" signifies participation in the very nature of divine glory. Various terms in John's gospel are also closely related—e.g., "He who has seen me has seen the Father" (Jn. 14, 9). Note also John 1, 18 and his whole prologue. It is not clear why the author of this gospel avoids the term *eikon*.[14]

### The New Man as the Image of God or Christ

The first important text is 2 Corinthians 3, 18. This verse is part of a traditional midrash which Paul uses as the basis for his considerations in verses 14-18, but we cannot recon-

---

[14] According to R. Bultmann in *Das Evangelium des Johannes* (Göttingen, 1957), p. 56, the author avoids the term *eikon* because of its cosmological connotations.

struct the midrash in detail.[15] It seems probable, however, that verse 18 is heavily impregnated with traditional elements. This is suggested by the somewhat atypical vocabulary which Paul uses,[16] the close tieup of the verse with the midrashic elements,[17] and especially the notion of transformation taking place here and now. As verse 18a indicates, the image into which we are being changed is the glory of the Lord.

Here the notion of *eikon* could simply mean "appearance" or "shape" in a neutral sense, but it seems more probable that it is used in a titular sense, referring to Christ as it does in 2 Corinthians 4, 4. The change going on is the here-and-now transformation of the faithful into the likeness of Christ which, according to verse 17, is identical with the Spirit. The Spirit (*pneuma*) is the "personal power of the risen one which serves as the medium of encounter and communication between the Lord and the Christian".[18]

Transformation, then, is achieved through the Spirit. For the community, the Spirit is the locus where it experiences the glorification that is taking place here and now in it through Christ.[19] The goal of this process is the *eikon*—that is, the likeness of Christ's glory. Through the Spirit, the faithful participate in his glory, which itself is Spirit. The weight of experience is focused on the present in this community, although this does not rule out an openness to the future.

We can probe further with the aid of Colossians 3, 19. The

[15] See the remarks in Luz, *op. cit.*, pp. 128ff.

[16] *Katoptrizo* and the other words derived from midrash are not Pauline.

[17] Note the perduring glory of *apo doksis eis doksan* over against the passing glory of Moses, the contrast between veiled and unveiled, and the mention of a bodily transformation of Moses in Philo, *Vit. Mos.* 2, 69.

[18] I. Hermann, *Kyrios und Pneuma* (Munich, 1961), p. 120.

[19] In this connection see the interesting phrase which Paul uses for exhortatory purposes: "He who cleaves to the Lord is *one* spirit with him" (1 Cor. 6, 17). Also note the notion of the body of Christ, which apparently derives from Corinthian theology and was adopted in a much more limited sense by Paul; it gives us some idea how the faithful, who are taken into Christ's body through the gift of the Spirit, participate in this glory.

text begins with an exhortation, but then focuses directly on baptism as the locus of salvation. It is in baptism that we have put off the old man and put on the new man which is being renewed in knowledge. Verse 10 contains traditional notions about baptism, even though we can no longer clearly distinguish between the traditional formulas and those of the author himself. The participles are not imperatives but real participles, as those in Colossians 2, 11ff. referring back to baptism.[20]

Several exegetical questions call for clarification. Who is the "new man" that Christians have put on at baptism? In my opinion, the participial phrase "which is being renewed" allows us to answer this question. It is not Christ [21] or the body of Christ, the Church, [22] which the baptized person now enters; it is the individual who is reborn in baptism (see also 2 Cor. 4, 16).

A more difficult question is what the phrase "after the image" refers to. It seems most clearly explicable if we make this phrase dependent on "which is being renewed", so that only "in knowledge" seems to be at variance with the ordinary terminology of the author. "Knowledge" here means an all-embracing knowledge of both God's will and his salvation plan. Thus in baptism the new man is renewed, and he continues to be renewed from then on "in the image of his creator". The creator here must be God, not Christ the co-creator of verses 15ff.[23]

Is *eikon* a reference to the *locus classicus of* man's likeness to God (i.e., Gen. 1, 26f.), or does it refer to the true *eikon* of God, Jesus Christ, mentioned in verses 15ff.? It is a moot question. The parallel text in Ephesians 4, 24 supports the first

[20] See Jervell, *op. cit.*, pp. 235f.

[21] Against this idea are several factors. Apart from *anaksinoumenon*, there is the prepositional phrase (*kat' eikona*) reminiscent of Genesis 1, 27, and the genitive *tou ktisantos*, whereby Christ is expressly designated as co-creator in Colossians 1.

[22] This tieup would fit best in verse 11, or in Ephesians 2, 15. Against it, however, is the notion of "putting on", and the contrast between the old man and the final phrase of verse 11.

[23] *Ktizo* is otherwise used by Paul only in reference to God; see also Eph. 2, 10; 3, 9; 4, 24.

possibility. Reference to Christ is there, in any case, by virtue of the mention of baptism. The new man is being renewed in the image of the creator because he has been baptized in the name of Jesus Christ; in baptism he has put off the old man, which apparently is not in the image of the creator. In short, *only the person who is baptized and incorporated into Christ's body can be regarded as the image of God; only he is renewed in God's likeness.*

We find other clear evidences of older tradition in verse 11, where we read: "Here there cannot be Greek and Jew, circumcised and uncircumcised, barbarian, Scythian, slave, freeman; but Christ is all, and in all." This enumeration seems to shoot beyond the context here.[24] The very similar text in Galatians 3, 27 makes it likely that here we are dealing with a pre-Pauline, "enthusiastic" interpretation of the new creation that has come about through baptism.[25] The likeness of God is clearly specified by verse 11: it is not the old world, but the new man who lives in the Christian community where differences no longer exist.

Romans 8, 29 also seems to go back to older traditions. The exact historical relationship of these traditional elements is complicated. The "golden thread" of Romans 8, 28. 30 suggests that Paul, or the community before him, wove a traditional piece into the text. God has predestined them and conformed them to the image of his Son. The affinity of this text to Colossians 1, 15 suggests that it, too, stems from a baptismal liturgy. When the text talks about the community's conformity to the *eikon,* God's Son, is it referring to a future glorification (as Paul certainly thought), or to a glorification already taking place in the present (cf., for example, 2 Cor. 3, 18; Col. 3, 10; compare 2 Cor. 4, 16)? We cannot say for sure, but we do know that the *eikon* here is the risen Jesus, not the earthly Jesus.[26]

[24] See G. Klein, *Die zwölf Apostel* (Göttingen, 1961), p. 195.
[25] See also P. Stuhlmacher, "Erwägungen zum ontologischen Charakter der *kaine ktisis* bei Paulus," in *Ev. Theol.* 27 (1967), pp. 1-35.
[26] Cf. W. Thüsing, *Per Christum in Deum* (Münster, 1965), pp. 126f.

Thus in the pre-Pauline community the notion of *eikon* played a central role. *Christ is the eikon of God; he is divine in nature and the only access to the unknown God.* Those baptized in his name gain a share in his nature and even now are being renewed after the *eikon* of God. This renewal is effected by the Spirit, who is given as a gift in baptism. *Thus we can speak about man's likeness to God only in connection with the mediating role of Christ. Any likeness of God in natural man is ruled out in this theology.* The old man has already been put aside.

### III

#### PAUL'S INTERPRETATION OF THIS THEOLOGY

Paul basically adds three emphases that alter the *eikon* theology of the pre-Pauline community.

### Glorification as a Future Process

Paul stresses the future nature of our glorification and conformity to Christ. This is clear in Philippians 3, 21—a text which Paul himself formulated even though he utilized traditional motifs.[27] As 1 Corinthians 15, 50ff. shows, Paul pictures the future transformation in a way similar to apocalyptic literature (e.g., *syr. Bar.* 51). Paul's view in 1 Corinthians 15, 49 is that we do not yet wear the heavenly *eikon,* although we already have borne the *eikon* of the earthly Adam. The line of thought here does not argue from Christ as the *eikon* of God or from Genesis 1, 26f. Its import is clear: the earthly and the heavenly exclude each other; if the future heavenly man wears the image of God, this means that he does not wear the image of the earthly man who is passing away.

[27] E. Guttgemann, *Der leidende Apostel und sein Herr* (Göttingen, 1960) prefers to see a traditional formula in Philippians 3, 20f. (pp. 240ff). On this interpretation, see Luz, *op. cit.,* p. 312 (footnote 53); also cf. J. Gnilka, *Der Philipperbrief* (Freiburg-Basel-Vienna, 1968), pp. 208f.

## The Reality of Suffering

Over against the idea of here-and-now transformation (e.g., 2 Cor. 3, 18) Paul sets the reality of suffering. We find a clear example of this in 2 Corinthians 4. Paul has talked about the traditional view of our transformation "from glory to glory" (3, 18) and about the proclamation of the Lord's Gospel (4, 1ff.). Then he goes on to show where this leads the Christian. He becomes a servant for Christ's sake (4, 5), so that the treasure of the Gospel is held in earthen vessels and Christ's life is revealed in our mortal flesh (4, 11).

This same cross-centered focus on the reality of suffering and death is apparent in Romans 8. His triumphant talk about the glorious transformation already underway (Rom. 8, 28ff.) is a counterpoint to his equally serious talk about the futility of the world (Rom. 8, 18ff.). The latter is a truly Pauline notion, and we can understand the former idea only in connection with it.

## Exhortatory Words

Finally there is the use of exhortation and admonition, which is clear in Colossians and Ephesians (Col. 3, 12ff.; Eph. 4, 22ff.), and which is quite in accord with Pauline theology. The author of Colossians appeals to the reality of the new man in baptism and the elimination of all differences in the community (3, 10-11) as the basis for an exhortation. The old differences have been taken away, so act accordingly! Even the triumphal hymn of Colossians ends with an exhortation (1, 23).

Thus we come to the close of our inquiry and we can attempt a summation. Paul does not discuss or consider any general likeness of God in man *in his soteriology,* nor do the communities which he served. Paul does bring up this notion once, in connection with the male! But he does this in an exhortatory context that has close ties with the exegetical tradition of the rabbis. However, he does not talk about man's likeness to God in general when it is a question of justification and redemption. In this context, Christ is the only *eikon* of God. Through baptism, the believer gains a share in this likeness to God. But it is effected paradoxically by suffering, positively by exhortation and admonition, and visibly only in the eschatological future. If Paul were to talk about some likeness to God outside of the *eikon,* Christ, this would mean that he believed in divine justification outside of Christ.

Stanislas Lyonnet, S.J./*Rome, Italy*

# The Presence of Christ and His Spirit in Man

In the Old Testament the "divine presence" is already seen as characteristic of "God's covenant with his people", so much so that the whole covenant relationship is expressed by this dwelling of God among men (Ex. 25, 8; Num. 35, 34; etc.). Yet, as we shall see, the Old Testament itself announced a special presence of God in the messianic community and in each of its members "at the end of time". This presence was certainly experienced, particularly by Paul, as perhaps the most significant new element in the Christian revelation.

## I

There is no doubt that this was the basic experience of Paul from the day of his conversion. The allusion to this event in Galatians already suggests this if the translation that seems most probable to me is the correct one: "Then God, who had specially chosen me while I was still in my mother's womb, called me through his grace and chose to reveal his Son *in me*" (1, 16). In any case, the bold confidence which runs through Philippians leaves no doubt whatever (3, 4-12). There Paul tells us not only how much his conversion constituted a break with his Judaistic past but also in what this break exactly consisted. For Christ's sake he "accepted the loss of everything" (v. 8); he renounced all the advantages which until then he had thought to be factors that assured his salvation: belonging to the chosen race through birth and circumcision, and the faultless observation of the law (v. 6), where "he stood out among other Jews", as he says in Galatians 1, 14. But it was thus that he "gained Christ". By "no longer trying for perfection by my own effort", a perfection which came from the law given by God for that purpose as he first thought, he now "wanted only the perfection that comes through faith in Christ, and is from God and based on faith" (v. 9).

This perfection was no longer essentially the fruit of his own actions, but presupposed that an Other had died and risen for him, and shared his own risen life with him, only asking that he accept this life by a free act of his own. This act was the act of faith as Paul understood it. In v. 10 he describes it as knowing "Christ and the power of his resurrection and the share in his sufferings". Paul "experienced" this power of the dead and risen Christ whose life had become his own. "Assimilated to the death of Christ", which Paul saw essentially as a supreme act of love, he already shared in Christ's resurrection through which he could leave the company of the dead in order to lead a "new life with Christ (Rom. 6, 4), a life essentially identical with that of the glorified Christ (cf. Col. 3, 1), though not flowering in its eternal glory".[1]

In the same epistle he said: "Life to me, of course, is Christ" (Phil. 1, 21), and he put it still more clearly in the epistle to the Galatians: "I have been crucified with Christ, and I live now not with my own life but with the life of Christ who lives in me" (2, 20). The context refers once again to the anti-Judaizing controversy. To the concept of a justification thought of as a gift of God, but also as something achieved by man through the observance of a law imposed from outside and "engraved on tablets of stone", Paul opposed a dispensation where

[1] Cf. J. Huby, *Epîtres de la captivité*, p. 348.

man is justified insofar as his own life becomes that of Christ, a life which, Paul stresses once again, he has accepted and made his own in some way "through faith in the Son of God who loved me and sacrificed himself for my sake" (2, 20b).

Now Paul does not hesitate to apply to all Christians what he has said about his own experience. One of the essential and most frequently mentioned thoughts in his writing is the union, and even identification, of the Christian with Christ, in the sense just described. The expressions vary. One of these is the formula "in Christ Jesus" or its equivalents. Though practically absent from the other writings of the New Testament, including the epistle to the Hebrews, it occurs more than 160 times in the thirteen Pauline epistles, with shades of meaning according to the context, which are not always easy to assess with any certainty.

Another formula, equally typical of Paul, is the description of the ecclesial community as the "body of Christ". This phrase is meant to express the mystery of the union between Christ and the Christians, which is the foundation of the unity of the Church and of Christians.

Paul did not develop this formula immediately. For instance, in Galatians 3, 27-28, he expressed that same twofold unity without referring to the image of the body: all those who are baptized form "one single living entity" (heis, in the masculine) with Christ, and, as St. John Chrysostom adds, in a union which is closer than if they formed one body.[2] In 1 Corinthians and Romans Paul adopted the well-known moral comparison used in the Hellenistic world for the same purpose. The profane authors used it to illustrate "the idea of interdependence and solidarity between different elements within a certain unity", and this unity was merely a moral unity. However, in Paul the comparison with the body is also used to explain the unity of each Christian with Christ (1 Cor. 6, 15-17; 10, 17). In 1 Corinthians 12, 12 and 27, Paul even seems

[2] St. John Chrysostom, *Hom. 9 on the Epistle to the Ephesians* (where he comments on Ephesians 4, 3): *P.G.* 62, col. 72.

to identify the local community with the person of Christ: this community forms "a body which is Christ" (*soma Christou,* with the genitive of definition), and "each of you is a different part of it" (27b). It would be hard to stress the immanence of Christ in the Church more powerfully, and perhaps even at the expense of his transcendence, the more so since during the same period the Stoics—as can be seen in a letter from Seneca to his friend Lucilius—also maintained in a more or less pantheistic sense that "the whole which contains us is God: we are part of it, we are the members". Or again: "This universe, which you observe, contains all beings, human and divine, and it is one: we are the members of a vast body." [3] In any case, in Romans 12, 5 Paul slightly modified the formula: "So all of us, in union with Christ, form one body, and as parts of it we belong to each other."

The final formula, "the body of Christ" (with two articles: *to soma tou Christou*), appeared in the epistles to the Colossians (1, 18. 24) and the Ephesians (4, 12). The Church, the whole of the Church, forms such an intimate unity with the risen Christ that one must express it by the unity which exists between the human person and his body. Here the transcendence of Christ is fully maintained, first of all, by the fact that "I am not my body", and then, in the same epistles, by the special place reserved for Christ—namely, that of the head (Col. 1, 18; 2, 19; Eph. 1, 23; etc.).

Finally, in Ephesians 1, 23 Paul explains in greater detail the metaphor of the head and the body as applied to the Church with the help of another idea—namely, that of "fullness", added by way of apposition. The Church is the "fullness of Christ", which means that she is filled with Christ, as Christ himself is filled with God—at least this seems the most probable sense to me—precisely as Paul explains in Colossians 2, 9 that "the fullness of divinity dwells in Christ", and that "in him all Christians are associated with this plenitude". In other words, all that is in God is in Christ and all that is in Christ is in the

[3] Seneca, *Letter to Lucilius* 92, 30 and 95, 52.

Church, the body of Christ. The relationship between the Church and Christ is analogous to that between Christ and the Father. In the same way we see in the fourth gospel that Christ invokes his relationship with the Father whenever he explains the relationship of Christians with himself: "My sheep know me as my Father knows me and I know the Father" (10, 14-5); "I am in my Father and you in me and I in you" (14, 20); "Father, may they be one in us, as you are in me and I am in you . . . that they may be one as we are one, with me in them and you in me" (17, 21-23).

For both Paul and John this presence of Christ in the Church and in every Christian is linked with the active presence of the Spirit. It is this presence of the Spirit which makes every Christian a son of God in the true sense of the word and allows him to address God in the same way, "Abba, Father", as the only Son (Gal. 4, 6; Rom. 8, 14-15). Christ's prayer becomes that of the Christian because in reality it is Christ who, in the Spirit, prays to the Father in each of us, just as it is Christ who loves his fellow men and his Father in the same Spirit. Thus Paul could write to the Romans that "the love of God—the love with which God loves us—has been poured into our hearts by the Spirit which has been given us" (5, 5). St. Augustine always had a particular liking for this verse and saw in it, quite rightly, the affirmation of the presence of God's love in our hearts through the love of the brother. He refers to it, for instance, when, in commenting on 1 John 3, 24, he states that "we know that he lives in us by the Spirit that he has given us", and shows that "the work of the Spirit in man is precisely to stir up in him the love of brotherly love (*dilectio caritatis*)".[4]

In the same way Paul also said of himself and his fellow workers in the apostolic field: "The love of Christ urges us" (2 Cor. 5, 14a). That love by which Christ loved us to the degree that he died for us (cf. v. 14b) "presses" the apostle

[4] St. Augustine, *On the First Epistle of St. John 6, 9* (*Sources Chrétiennes* 75, p. 6).

and holds him, as it were, in a vise, pulling him out of himself in order to give himself to the work to which Christ had called him, the work which God entrusted to his Son and which must be fulfilled, the "reconciliation of the world" (vv. 18-20). Moreover, Paul seems to give the Greek verb *synechein,* translated as "urging" or "pressing", the meaning which it had acquired in popular philosophy, such as it occurs in the passage of Wisdom where the Spirit of the Lord is said "to hold all things together by filling the universe" (Wis. 1, 7)—the function which the Stoics attributed to that fluid force immanent in the world for which they used the word "spirit" and which the author of Wisdom attributed to Yahweh's own Spirit. It is this function which Paul attributes to that "love of God, poured into our hearts by the Spirit which has been given us." It is this love which later theology will describe as "theological" because it "unites us directly with God" [5]—that is, with what, if one may use the expression, is most God in God, since "God is love" (1 Jn. 4, 8).

## II

As I said at the beginning, in this active presence of Christ and the Spirit in man, Paul saw something so radically new that his conversion implied a real break with Judaism as he had practiced it. But he could not fail to see that this was also the fulfillment of what the Old Testament had announced for the messianic age.

The Old Testament indeed frequently mentioned a covenant of the future (from Hosea 2, 16-25 on), a covenant of peace (e.g., Is. 54, 10), an eternal covenant (cf. Is. 55, 3; Jer. 32, 40; Ezek. 37, 26), a new covenant (Jer. 31, 31). This last passage, the only one where the expression "the new covenant"

---

[5] This is the definition of a "theological virtue" given by St. Thomas in his remarks on 1 Corinthians 13, 13; cf. his *Commentary on 1 Cor. 13,* lect. 4 (ed. R. Cai, n. 805).

occurs in the Old Testament, and to which the New Testament and Qumran texts refer, even contrasts this covenant in detail with the old one. Both are defined, in Jewish fashion, by "the gift of the law", the *mattan torah*. But while on Mount Sinai God had promulgated his law, the expression of his will, as a norm imposed on man from outside, Jeremiah declared: "No, this is the covenant I will make with the house of Israel when those days arrive—it is Yahweh who speaks. Deep within them I will plant my law, writing it on their hearts. Then I will be their God and they will be my people" (Jer. 31, 33).

God will therefore not be satisfied with a law promulgated from outside, as laws are usually promulgated, but will put it right within man, and not written on tablets of stone (cf. Ex. 32, 16), but on the heart of every Israelite. The mediation of a mere man like Moses would not be enough for that. This interior renewal demanded a personal intervention by God in each member of the messianic community. This is what Deuteronomy had foretold in different terms when, instead of summing up the whole law in the single precept: "Circumcise your heart" (Dt. 10, 16), it says that in the future "Yahweh your God will circumcise your heart and the heart of your descendants, until you love Yahweh your God with all your heart and soul, and so have life" (Dt. 30, 6). Then there is Ezekiel, who, some twenty years after Jeremiah, took up the formula coined by his predecessor and substituted the term "spirit" for "law": "I shall give you a new heart, and put a new spirit in you . . . I shall put my spirit in you" (Ezek. 36, 26-27). The gift of "the law engraved on the heart" is identical with the gift of Yahweh's own Spirit.

The conclusion is clear: If God's law has become so much something in man himself, and God's Spirit has become the very principle of our moral conduct, our conduct will necessarily be consistent with God's law (that is, his will) in the degree in which man achieves this interior assimilation, even though this will only be complete in heaven. And this is what Jeremiah said: "Then there will be no further need for neighbor to try to teach neighbor, or brother to say to brother, 'Learn to know Yahweh.' No, they will all know me, the least no less than the greatest" (Jer. 31, 33-34). And Ezekiel states it more clearly still: "I shall put my spirit inside you, and make you keep my laws and sincerely respect my observances" (Ezek. 36, 27).

"They will no longer have to teach each other" because God himself will be their master, a master who intends to be present and to act upon man from within. This theme is a common one in the Bible (cf. Is. 48, 17; 54, 13 [quoted in Jn. 6, 45]; 55, 1-3; Dt. 8, 2; Ps. 32, 8; etc.). A variation on this theme occurs in Proverbs 9, 2-6 ("Wisdom has laid her table. . . . Come and eat my bread, drink the wine I have prepared. Leave your folly and you will live, walk in the ways of perception") and in Ecclesiasticus 24, 19-21 ("Approach me, you who desire me. . . . They who eat me will hunger for more, they who drink me will thirst for more"). All these expressions are echoed in the New Testament, which applies them to Christ sharing his life and his love with the Christians.

It has not been sufficiently realized how much the two oracles of Jeremiah and Ezekiel which proclaim this presence of God and his Spirit in man influenced and explained a number of things said by Paul and John. The direct or indirect references are quoted, such as John 6, 45, which refers to the parallel passage in Isaiah 54, 13, or 2 Corinthians 3, 3-7, which opposes the ministry of death, written on stones, to the ministry of the Spirit, and is explicitly linked up with "the new covenant". But it is perhaps not often pointed out that the epistle to the Romans takes up this opposition between "the old letter" and the "new Spirit", first in 2, 29, in connection with the pagans who observe the commandments of the law without understanding them, and then in 7, 6, which introduces the development of chapter 8 about the Christian life understood as a life in the Spirit.

In actual fact, Paul directly refers to these two prophecies in a very significant passage of his first epistle to the Thessalonians (4, 8-9), in which he reminds them of "the instructions he has given them about the kind of life that God wants" and which they already observe in their conduct (v. 1) not only in the sense that their sanctification is willed by God, but also in the sense that "the will of God achieves sanctity", as the Jerusalem Bible observes in a note, and as Paul said in his second epistle to them: "God chose you from the beginning to be saved by the sanctifying Spirit" (2 Thess. 2, 13). And so the apostle adds that "anyone who objects" to being sanctified in this way "is not objecting to a human authority, but to God, who gives you his Holy Spirit" (v. 8). Such a refusal is therefore not simply disobeying a commandment, not even a commandment given by God himself, but obstructing God's activity operating in the very heart of the Christian through the gift of his Spirit. The present participle (*ton kai didonta*), which the editors have preferred to the aorist participle, underlines the continuity of this activity of God as he operates at the heart of our being through his Spirit, as Ezekiel had already prophesied for the messianic age.

The following verse refers no less clearly to Jeremiah's saying about the gift of a law written on man's heart through which men no longer need to be instructed by each other, since they are directly taught by God: "As for loving the brother, there is no need for anyone to write to you about that, since you have learned from God yourselves to love one another" (v. 9). The Thessalonians have not simply learned the existence of a divine precept commanding them to love the neighbor, but God has taught them to love one another by putting his law (Jeremiah), his own Spirit (Ezekiel), in the very ground of their being. In other words, God shares his own love with them through Christ in the Spirit, so that each of them can say with St. Paul: "It is no longer I that love but Christ who loves in me" (cf. Gal. 2, 20).

Once we see this, we can understand without difficulty why, in Galatians, Paul bases the filiation of the Christian, and therefore his freedom, on the gift of the Spirit (Gal. 4, 6-7; Rom.

8, 14-15), the characteristic feature of the "new covenant", just as the filiation and freedom of Israel were based on the first covenant, of which the characteristic feature is the gift of the law.[6] It will be equally clear that this freedom of the Christian is essentially and simultaneously a being freed from the law and the fulfillment of the law, as Paul explains in Romans 8, 2-4. It is true that more than one scholar still finds this a difficult passage, but the meaning becomes clear when we see there, as it were, a résumé of Jeremiah 31, 33 and Ezekiel 36, 27.

Verse 2 says first that the Christian has been set free by what Paul calls "the law of the Spirit of life" (i.e., with the genitive of definition), "the law which is the Spirit", the law written on the heart, as announced by Jeremiah 31, 33, identified with Yahweh's own Spirit by Ezekiel (36, 37) whose vision of the dry bones (37, 1-14) shows how this Spirit is able to give life. Verse 4 then sets out God's aim in putting his Spirit in the ground of our being: ". . . that the commandment of the law may be fulfilled in us." This is therefore the law to which Jeremiah and Ezekiel referred. But Paul here purposely uses some very careful wording, and there are two expressions that deserve scrutiny. First, instead of using the usual plural, the "commandments of the law", he uses the singular, the "commandment of the law", because "one single precept contains the whole law in its fullness", as he had said in Galatians 5, 14 and as he would repeat it in Romans 13, 8-10. Then, and especially, he puts the verb in the passive mood ("the commandment is fulfilled") because in his eyes this fulfillment is much less our effort than that of the Spirit, "who, creating in us that love of the neighbor, the fullness of the law, is the new covenant".[7]

In St. John we find exactly the same teaching, although he uses different terms. The importance of the gift of the Spirit in the fourth gospel is well known. In the prologue Christ is

[6] Cf. Ex. 4, 22-23; Lev. 26, 13, where the Septuagint even has the term *parrhesia*. The Passover is still preeminently the feast of freedom for the Jews.

[7] St. Thomas, *On 2 Cor. 3*, lect. 2 (ed. R. Cai, n. 90).

presented as the one from whom "grace and truth have come" (1, 17). As John the Baptist explains, this is the one who will "take away the sin of the world" by "baptizing in the Spirit" (1, 29. 33), a mission which the evangelist develops in detail throughout his narrative, from the mysterious allusion to the "spiritual temple" (2, 19)—from which a source of living water will spring forth (4, 10. 14), with a reference to Ezekiel (47, 1f.), and explicitly identified with the Spirit Christ will will send after his glorification (7, 37-39)—up to the unusual formula with which the death of Christ is described as the "giving up of the spirit" (19, 30). By this phrase John meant that "the last breath of Jesus foreshadows the pouring out of the Spirit" (Jerusalem Bible). This is clearly emphasized by the episode of the pierced side "out of which came blood and water", a double allusion to the first Easter and the prophecy of Zechariah: "When that day comes, a fountain will be opened for the house of David and the citizens of Jerusalem, for sin and impurity" (13, 1; cf. 14, 8 and Ezek. 47, 1f.). Jesus is in truth the "Lamb of God who takes away the sin of the world by baptism in the Spirit", as John the Baptist said. Finally, on the evening of Easter day, Christ would give his Church the same power to give the Spirit for the remission of sins (Jn. 20, 22).

But the allusion to both Ezekiel and Jeremiah becomes as clear in the first epistle of John as it was in Paul. Boismard has pointed out: "In this letter John deliberately presented the relations between God and men as the fulfillment of the prophecies of Jeremiah and Ezekiel about the new convenant." [8] More recently, de la Potterie, in his study of 1 John 2, 12-14, expressed the opinion that "practically all the details of these verses have some point of contact with one or other of these two prophetic texts".[9]

In fact, it is not merely a matter of a single passage, but

[8] M. Boismard, "La connaissance dans l'alliance nouvelle, d'après la première lettre de saint Jean," in *Rev. Biblique* 56 (1949), p. 388.

[9] I. de la Potterie, "La connaissance de Dieu dans le dualisme eschatologique d'après 1 Jn. 2, 12-14," in *Au service de la parole de Dieu*, p. 87.

of the whole epistle, and these two texts throw a new light on all its main statements. For instance, 2, 20 reads: "But you have been anointed by the Holy One, and have all received the knowledge." And 2, 27 states: "But you have not lost the anointing that he gave you, and you do not need anyone to teach you: the anointing he gave you teaches you everything." And still more strongly, 5, 20 declares: "We know that the Son of God has come, and has given us the understanding (*ten dianoian*) so that we may know the true One." Boismard quite correctly compares this text with Jeremiah 24, 7: "I will give them a heart to know that I am Yahweh. They shall be my people and I will be their God, for they will return to me with all their heart." The term *dianoia* (understanding), which occurs only here in John, corresponds to the *kardia* (heart) of Jeremiah. But the correspondence of this use with that in Jeremiah 31, 33 is no less striking when we look at the Septuagint translation which states: "I shall put my laws in their *dianoia* (the only passage where the Hebrew term is thus translated) and I shall write them on their *kardia*." If the Christian "knows God" (2, 3; 4, 7-8; 5, 20), "observes his commandments" (2, 3), "does not sin" (3, 5-6) and "conducts himself as Christ conducted himself" (2, 6), according to the commandment which is both old and new (2, 7; cf. Jn. 13, 15. 34), it is because "God dwells in him and he dwells in God" (2, 3; 3, 5. 24; 4, 13), "the anointing given by the Holy One remains in him" and "teaches him everything" (2, 27), "God has given him his Spirit" (3, 24; 4, 13), and "God's love comes to perfection in him" (2, 5).

It is therefore clear that for both John and Paul the presence of God in man through Christ in the Spirit really constitutes the essence of that message of salvation which Christ charged his apostles to proclaim to the world. Thus this is probably the full meaning of the phrase used by Paul in his epistle to the Colossians, "Christ in you" (Col. 1, 27). It undoubtedly means that the message, first reserved for Israel, is now preached also to the pagans, but at the same time it specifies the content of this message (Christ, the only source of salvation for both Jews and pagans, is henceforth your life, shares with you his Spirit, the Spirit of God himself, and enables you through this presence in the ground of your being to "lead a life worthy of the Lord" and to fulfill his will (Col. 1, 9-10). In concrete terms this means "to love one another as Christ has loved you". Without doubt this is also the full meaning of the confession of faith mentioned, for instance, in Romans 10, 9: "If your lips confess that Jesus is Lord and if you believe in your heart that God raised him from the dead, then you will be saved." To proclaim the lordship of Christ and his resurrection from the dead is not merely asserting Christ's divinity and the historical reality of a past event, but also, as Paul did according to Festus (Acts 25, 9), that "a dead man called Jesus is alive today"—alive, no doubt, "at the right hand of the Father" where he does not cease to "intercede for us" (Rom. 8, 34), but is alive in his Church and in the heart of every disciple.

This active presence dominates the Christian's moral conduct, his behavior and his *peripatein* (walking) throughout life, and therefore demands constant docility. It also necessarily requires that we accept and cooperate with this activity which is going on at the very root of our freedom. As Paul states: "The commandment of the law is fulfilled in us who do not live according to our unspiritual nature but according to the Spirit" (Rom. 8, 4). And the following verses show that the Christian cannot maintain this docility to the Spirit without a constant struggle, as Paul had said in Galatians 5, 17-24. For the Christian can cease to be "animated by the Spirit" and will have to undergo the consequences: "If you live according to your unspiritual nature, you are doomed to die" (Rom. 8, 13a). Paul even talks of "mortification": "If by the Spirit you put an end to the misdeeds of the body—the actions of the 'old man' who reasserts himself constantly in us—you will live" (v. 13b). In the same way he had warned the Galatians: "You cannot belong to Christ Jesus unless you crucify all self-indulgent passions and desires" (Gal. 5, 24). But we should not forget that this "mortification" and this "crucifixion" are still the work of the Spirit in us, not of the law. All that the Christian does—particularly in the faith, of which baptism is the sacrament, and in the exercise of the Christian virtues, especially brotherly love, of which the eucharist is the sacrament —is thus directed toward the reception and maintenance of the active presence of Christ and the Spirit in us.

Jerome Murphy-O'Connor, O.P./*Jerusalem, Israel*

# The Presence of God through Christ in the Church and in the World

The ambiguities and nuances of the concept of "presence" have been thrown into relief by contemporary concern with community and interpersonal relations.[1] Clarity demands that we distinguish between physical and personal presence. Both are based on some form of communication, but while any direct action is sufficient to create the first type, mutual self-revelation is the indispensable and only condition of the second. Lovers are permanently present to each other in a personal way, even when separated in place and time.

The problem of God's presence, therefore, can be considered on two different levels. The traditional category of "omnipresence" is concerned with divine presence on the physical level. God is present everywhere because, as first cause, he influences all things directly. True as it is, this concept of the divine presence exercises little attraction today. In a world which is passing from the ontological to the functional period of its history the question "Does God exist?" really means: "Can God be personally present to me as a friend?" Neither the five ways of Saint Thomas nor the numerous affirmations of both

[1] This became particularly clear in the debate regarding the real presence; cf. P. Schoonenberg, "The Real Presence in Contemporary Discussion," in *Theol. Digest* 15 (1967), pp. 3-11; E. Schillebeeckx, *Die eucharistische Gegenwart* (Düsseldorf, 1967).

the Old and New Testaments concerning God's omnipresence [2] constitute an adequate answer to this question. They do convey a valid insight, but it is on a different level to that on which the question is posed. Nor is it sufficient to try to adapt the "omnipresence" answer to the question by saying that once God's physical presence is recognized it becomes personal presence. Such an effort reveals a complete misunderstanding of the nature of personal presence in which there is much that transcends the purely intellectual dimension.

In order to appreciate the full implications of the crucial question "Can God be personally present to me?" it must be recognized that it embodies a more fundamental query: "Has God offered his friendship to men?" These two questions command the structure of this inquiry into Saint Paul's understanding of God's personal presence. The first part examines the ontological possibility of this presence in terms of the apostle's view of Christ as the self-revealing invitation of the Father. For the contemporaries of Jesus, contact with him created the ontic possibility of God's personal presence, since in his person he represented God's openness even to those who had repudiated his friendship through sin.[3] But how was this ontic possibility to be realized in the post-paschal period? Paul does not formulate this question explicitly, but the nature of his mission obliged him to give thought to the problem of communicating his faith. Hence the second part of this article endeavors to draw together those texts which suggest that the offer of God's presence only becomes an ontic possibility if Christians are, collectively and individually, other Christs. Particularly in this second part will we find the insights that throw light on the problems presently confronting the Church.

[2] E.g., Jer. 23, 24; Is. 6, 3; Col. 1, 19.
[3] For the distinction between ontological and ontic possibility, cf. J. Macquarrie, *An Existentialist Theology* (London, 1960), pp. 30-31.

## I
### JESUS CHRIST: THE INVITATION OF THE FATHER

The center of Paul's teaching is Christ. "Everything con-
verges on this point; thence everything procedes, and thither
everything returns." [4] Of course, this is not to say that God is
ignored. In the dogmatic part of Romans, for example, he is
mentioned three times more frequently than Christ. For Paul
theology and christology are one, because everything he wrote
is, in one form or another, a working out of his fundamental
intuition that God has revealed himself in Christ.

Personal presence is a mutual relationship based on a sign
in which one person reveals himself to the other. Unless the
sign (a word or gesture) is given and unless the other responds with a similar openness, there may be physical presence
of one to the other, but on the personal level there is nothing,
an absence. In establishing this relationship one of the parties
must take the initiative. Certain parts of the Old Testament seem
to imply that man must take the first step in reestablishing
a relationship with God that had been broken by sin, but
Jeremiah and Ezekiel recognized that this was impossible (Jer.
31, 18. 31-34; Ezek. 37, 14. 26). Paul shares their point of
view. His conception of unredeemed man reveals the mode of
being proper to the "old man" to be exclusively egocentric. If
left to himself man would never open himself to God. Hence
Paul continually emphasizes that the initiative is taken by the
Father. It is not man who from his misery appeals to God, but
God who motivated by love calls men to himself (2 Thess. 2,
13; etc.). This love is not drawn by anything in man, because
God has to make him worthy of his call (2 Thess. 1, 11).

Paul does not speculate on how this is possible. All his attention is concentrated on the mode of God's self-revelation.
In order to convince men of his openness to them, God had to

[4] F. Prat, *La théologie de saint Paul* II (Paris, 1938), p. 14.

bring himself within the orbit of their experience in such a way that this love for them became almost tangible. Hence, "God sent his Son, born of a woman" (Gal. 4, 4; Rom. 8, 3); "God shows his love for us in that while we were yet sinners Christ died for us" (Rom. 5, 8). No longer are God's power and wisdom revealed through an action such as the giving of the law on Sinai, but his love is made manifest in the sending of a person, Jesus Christ. The pastoral epistles may be Deutero-Pauline, but in certain instances they represent a homogeneous development of Pauline insights. This is certainly the case when Christ is presented as "the manifestation of the goodness and loving kindness of God" (Tit. 3, 4). Here the element of invitation implicit in Paul's formulations is brought clearly to the fore.

Jesus is not called "God" in the more primitive strata of the New Testament. Only toward the end of the 1st century did the title come into frequent usage. The earliest probable instance occurs in the Pauline epistles: "Of their race [i.e., the Israelites] is the Christ according to the flesh, who is over all, God blessed forever" (Rom. 9, 5).[5] R. Brown has suggested that two closely related factors contributed to this development.[6] The majority of the texts which call Jesus "God" originally had a liturgical *Sitz im Leben;* praise of Jesus in a context dedicated to the praise of God tended to narrow the gap between the two. Moreover, as the first Christians penetrated the mystery of Jesus they gradually realized how much of himself God had revealed in his Son, and this led to a broadening of the title "God" to include Father and Son.

This awareness of Christ's unique relationship to the Father is particularly marked in the christological hymn of Colossians 1, 15-20. For our purpose it is irrelevant whether the hymn is Pauline or not; its use by the apostle is sufficient evidence that

[5] This text is a famous crux, and there is no unanimity on its interpretation. At most it can be said that the punctuation adopted here does the least violence to grammar and New Testament usage.

[6] R. Brown, "Does the New Testament Call Jesus God?" in *Theol. Studies* 26 (1965), pp. 545-73.

the ideas it embodies harmonized with his own patterns of thought. The key insight of the hymn is the identification of Christ with Wisdom. Paul had already applied sapiential categories to Christ,[7] but had not fully exploited their possibilities. The sapiential texts which speak of the creative wisdom of God are best understood as expressions of awe at the thought of the unique creator of so many marvels. This view of reality is essentially optimistic. The world is not a frightening place into which man is thrown as into a sea of alien being. It is a place of wonder and beauty, because it is viewed in a perspective that gives it unity, meaning and purpose. For the sapiential writers this perspective was given by Wisdom; for the author of the hymn it is provided by Christ.

However, there is no parallel in the sapiential literature to the assertion of the hymn that Christ embodies the finality of the cosmos ("All things . . . to him have been created"—Col. 1, 17). Acceptance of this formulation marks an evolution in Paul's thought, which becomes evident if we compare 1 Corinthians 8, 6: "For us [there is but] one God, the Father, from whom [come] all things, and to whom we [go]; and one Lord, Jesus Christ, through whom [come] all things, and through whom we [go]." [8] Here *God* is the Alpha and Omega of everything that exists (cf. Is. 44, 6)—a commonplace in any theistic understanding of the world.

How is this to be reconciled with the role attributed to Christ by the hymn? One possibility is to see the hymn as an implicit affirmation of the divinity of Christ. This approach would give full value to the assertion that Christ is "the image of the invisible God" (Col. 1, 15). A second possibility which does not exclude the first, and which may be more probable if the hymn is pre-Pauline, is to see Christ as the perfect fulfillment of God's design for his creation, because in him God and man

[7] Cf. A. Feuillet, *Le Christ Sagesse de Dieu dans les épîtres pauliniennes* (Paris, 1966).

[8] For the justification of the verbs supplied to bring out the sense of this text, cf. F. Sagnard, "A propos de 1 Cor. 8, 6," in *Ephem. Theol. Lov.* 26 (1950), pp. 54-58.

are joined in total harmony. This second interpretation would seem to be confirmed by the second strophe where Stoic and sapiential categories are combined, because there we see that it is by reconciling a sin-divided cosmos through his Son that God causes it to dwell in Christ (Col. 1, 19-20). Thus, in addition to being God's invitation to the world, Christ also manifests the result of the acceptance of that invitation; the pristine harmony of the cosmos is restored.

In thus describing the reconciliation of all things as an already accomplished fact, Paul speaks with the certitude of optimism (compare the more realistic view of Rom. 8, 20-21). The idea of material realities as being in need of reconciliation is totally foreign to us, but Paul, in harmony with the Old Testament writers, viewed all created reality in a single perspective. In sinning, man upsets the delicate balance of the whole, and in certain cases he distorts the intrinsic finality of material entities (cf. Lv. 26, 33-35). It is he who creates the need for reconciliation, and the work of reconciliation is focused in and through him. By responding to God's invitation in Christ, man contributes to the restoration of the whole. In a sense he re-creates material reality. He draws everything he touches into his own theocentric finality. This insight into man's role as a prolongation of that of Christ leads naturally into the second part of this study.

## II

### THE WHOLE CHRIST

For all the clarity of his awareness of Christ as the self-revealing invitation of the Father, Paul never calls him the Word, as does St. John. Christ is the Word for those who experience him, who are fully conscious of who he is and what he means. But Paul's life was dedicated to those who did not know Christ, and his mission was to ensure the presence of Christ among them. Genuine confrontation with Christ is the only road to

faith and thus to the presence of God. Faith, however, involves a literally appalling decision.[9] The demand implicit in
the preaching is that one accept Jesus Christ as totally similar
to us (Jesus the man) and at the same time as totally "other"
(the risen Christ, the Savior). There is no security here, nothing
the intellect can firmly grasp. From any purely human point of
view it is simply "a stumbling block to Jews and folly to Gentiles" (1 Cor. 1, 23). One cannot even attach oneself to Jesus,
because the climax of the decision is baptism into his *death*
(Rom. 6, 3). Nothing human can adequately motivate this decision. Preaching can only bring man to the threshold. Its function is limited to clarifying the confrontation, but this confrontation with Christ can only take place when the Word is
proposed in such a way as to force man to consider two radically
different planes of experience ("Jesus" and "Christ") *to-*
*gether.* "Plausible words of wisdom" (1 Cor. 2, 4)—i.e. per-
suasive arguments—are totally inadequate because they era-
dicate the element of "otherness" that is of the very nature
of this confrontation. Simple affirmation is no better: "The kingdom of God does not come to be through words, but through
power" (1 Cor. 4, 20). Genuine faith "does not rest in the
wisdom of men but in the power of God" (1 Cor. 2, 5). This
power is released by the context in or from which the Word is
spoken, and which makes the element of "otherness" ines-
capable. Paul never formally defines this context, but various
indications scattered throughout his letters suggest that it is the
believing community.

Of the community at Corinth Paul says, "You yourselves are
our letter of recommendation written on your hearts to be read
and known by all men; and you show that you are a letter of
Christ delivered by us, written not with ink but with the spirit
of the living God, not on tablets of stone but on tablets of
human hearts" (2 Cor. 3, 2-3). Knowing the unhappy situation of the church at Corinth, one might suspect a touch of

[9] For a recent and biblically based analysis of the act of faith, cf. R.
Haughton, *The Act of Love* (London, 1968).

irony here, but even if Paul is speaking on the level of possibility, we have here an important insight into the role of the
Christian community. Its way of life should be an extension of
the invitation embodied in Christ. In Philippians this is defined as "a holding forth of the Word of life" (Phil. 2, 16). It
is clear from the context that it is not a question of verbal
proclamation. The influence of the believers, that which makes
them "shine as lights in the world", is the quality of their lives.
It would be an oversimplification to say that their obedience
enhances the credibility of the Word, and that this credibility
is its power. The Christian life lived in its fullness produces
an emotional shock on the uncommitted observer similar to that
produced by the resurrection on the first disciples. It attests
that the believers are no longer enmeshed in the limitations
that weigh upon him, that they have found a source of life
and strength whose need he now experiences more keenly than
ever before. Thus a receptivity to the Word is generated because it is demanded as an explanation. Hence it is natural to
find Paul thanking the Philippians for their "partnership (koinonia) in the spreading of the Gospel" (Phil. 1, 5).

The apostle never said anything like this to the Corinthians.
On the contrary he had to admonish them: "Strive not to be an
obstacle either to Jews or to Greeks or to the Church of God,
just as I, for my part, render service to all in everything. I
seek not what benefits myself but what benefits everyone else,
so that they may be saved. Become imitators of me, just as I
am an imitator of Christ" (1 Cor. 10, 31—11, 1). This text
is important because it introduces the themes of "obstacle" and
"imitation". We see here that a community can be a barrier
to faith. Most frequently this theme is referred to the person of
Paul. When he speaks of the possibility of his being an obstacle to the Word (1 Cor. 9, 12; 2 Cor. 6, 3; 11, 7), what
is uppermost in his mind is the question of his motivation. The
impact of his words would be greatly diminished were there
reason to suspect that he was acting from any motive other than
the need to communicate the tremendous experience he has un-

dergone in his encounter with Christ (2 Cor. 5, 14). Impeccable behavior stemming from a lesser motive would not ring true. His sensitivity on this point is so delicate that he has no need to speak of the adverse impact of un-Christian behavior. Despite its seeming arrogance, the exhortation "Become imitators of me" is only the other side of the same coin. Unless the apostle has truly "put on Christ" (Gal. 3, 7), unless he speaks as another Christ, he is incapable of confronting his hearers with Christ.

In Paul's theology the factor that enables the believer and the community to re-present Christ is the presence of the Spirit; both are temples in which the Spirit dwells (1 Cor. 3, 16-17; 6, 19). This is not a personal presence. Through the action of the Spirit God empowers man to realize the possibilities opened to humanity by Christ.[10] This is the ultimate source of the quality of "otherness" that should distinguish Christians both collectively and individually. This quality of "otherness" is sanctity, or transcendence made manifest.[11] It is impossible to define its component elements adequately, but Paul touches on one aspect of the problem when he speaks of the eucharist at Corinth.[12]

Ideally the eucharistic assembly should be a proclamation of the Lord's death (1 Cor. 11, 26). It should be a visible sign that God "loved us and sent his Son to be the expiation for our sins" (1 Jn. 4, 10). Paul's attention is focused primarily on the liturgical assembly as realizing the Father's invitation to personal presence, not on the real presence of Christ in the eucharist. The two aspects are intimately related, but the latter does not automatically imply the former, as Paul emphasizes: "When you meet together, it is not the Lord's supper that you eat, for in eating each one goes ahead with his own meal, and one is hungry and another is drunk" (1 Cor. 11, 20-21).

[10] Cf. W. Pfister, *Das Leben im Geist nach Paulus* (Freibourg, 1963).
[11] Cf. R. Latourelle, "La sainteté signe de la Révélation," in *Gregorianum* 46 (1965), pp. 36-65.
[12] Cf. L. Dequeker and W. Zuidema, "The Eucharist and St. Paul (1 Cor. 11, 17-34)," in *Concilium* 40 (1968), pp. 48-59.

The behavior of the Corinthians had nullified the revelatory character of the meal, so that Paul could say without equivocation that the meal the Corinthians ate was not the Lord's supper. Many unsuccessful attempts have been made to diminish the impact of this statement, but it is clear that for the apostle external appearances affect an essential dimension of the liturgical celebration.

In order to understand this we must recollect that the reconciliation effected by the death of Christ has both a vertical and a horizontal dimension: man is reconciled with God and with his fellow men. These cannot be separated because one is the condition of the other. Man's being is essentially social. His need for others and his dependence on them are so much a part of the structure of his being that he cannot develop normally as a person without them. Yet aggressiveness is equally a feature of human nature. Man feels himself threatened by the other and instinctively builds psychic, and even physical, defenses against intimacy. This tension—man needs to trust and yet he cannot—is perhaps the most painful evidence of his fallen state.

It is against this background that Paul's statement stands out in clearest relief. The eucharist is the sacrament of the reconciliation effected by Christ, and those who participate in it should manifest that this tension has *in fact* been resolved. A community in which complete peace and mutual confidence reign contrasts vividly with its environment; it has the quality of "otherness" that is the only appropriate setting for the Word. The eucharistic assembly is a contradiction in terms unless the participants are in fact reconciled with each other. Yet it should not be overlooked that at the same time the eucharist has a role to play in the creation of that union, since it includes both the vertical and horizontal dimensions: "The bread which we break, is it not communion (*koinonia*) in the body of Christ?" (1 Cor. 10, 26). It prolongs and intensifies the effects of baptism, whose social dimension is also strongly marked in the epistles: "You have put on the new man . . . *where* there can be no distinction between Greek and Jew, circumcised and uncircumcised, barbarian, Scythian, slave, freeman, but Christ is all, and in all" (Col. 3, 10-11). The "new man" is the whole Christ, head and members.

In the texts discussed above, Paul gives equal emphasis to the community and to the individual. Both can be signs or anti-signs.[13] As signs they are christological. If the Word spoken by the individual effects a real confrontation with Christ, it is because he is another Christ. If the community projects the Word of life, it is because it truly is the body of Christ. In both cases Paul's thought moves on the phenomenological level. He has in mind a perceptible quality that has the effect of transforming the causal presence of God in preaching and the liturgy into the ontic possibility of his personal presence. If, as we have seen, Christ is *the* invitation to this presence, he is also the paradigm of man's response. This appears most clearly in the "new Adam" texts where the obedience of the last Adam is contrasted with the disobedience of the first Adam (Rom. 5, 12-21).

These two figures represent the two strains of man's collective and individual heritage. In the present they are in tension, and the reality of the ontic possibility of God's presence is conditioned by the extent to which the influence of Christ prevails over that of Adam. Thus the image of Christ in the individual or the community is never perfect. A more perfect representation is always possible. "We all, with unveiled face reflecting the glory of the Lord, are being changed from glory to glory" (2 Cor. 3, 18). After his experience of God on Sinai, Moses' face was so radiant with reflected glory that he had to keep it veiled from his fellow Israelites. But this brightness, like the covenant it symbolized, was only transitory. The new covenant,

---

[13] For this theme in the pastoral epistles and in 1 Peter, cf. P. Lippert, *Lebens als Zeugnis: Die werbende Kraft christlicher Lebensführung nach dem Kirchenverständnis neutestamentlicher Briefe* (Stuttgart, 1968).

however, is symbolized by the glory of Christ. Because believers are formed in the image of Christ (Rom. 8, 29) they
are his glory. In both the Old and New Testaments, "glory"
denotes a visible, effective manifestation of God. Just as Christ
mediated the Father to men, so do the believers mediate Christ
to a generation that never knew him in the flesh. By "from glory
to glory" Paul simply means that the image of Christ in the
believer should become progressively more manifest. It would
be false to the apostle's essential realism to understand the image
of Christ in a mystical or static sense. To be transformed means
to have "the mind of Christ" (1 Cor. 2, 16; Phil. 2, 5; Rom.
15, 5), and, as Bultmann has pointed out, "mind" in these
contexts might almost be rendered by "character"—which is
formed and made manifest in one's way of being.

This dynamic element is more evident in a second text: "And
his gifts were that some should be apostles, some prophets,
some evangelists . . . for the building up of the body of Christ,
until we all, together, come to unity in faith and knowledge of
the Son of God, and constitute the perfect man, fully mature,
who realizes the plenitude of Christ" (Eph. 4, 11-13). The
conciseness and the profundity of this text make it difficult to
translate, and although another hand played a major role in
the formulation of Ephesians, the thought is fundamentally that
of Paul. As in 2 Corinthians, we are concerned with a process
of becoming. Until the end of time the body of Christ can be
built up both intensively and extensively. By striving together
toward ever more perfect unity in commitment and action, the
believers ("the new man") progressively bring into being "the
perfect man", who is the whole Christ in his plenitude.

Until this final moment the life of the Church is shrouded in
the same ambiguity that characterized the earthly life of Jesus. In
neither case is God's invitation so clear and forceful as to *demand*
acceptance. This would be contrary to the concept of personal
presence. Friendship is not demanded. The self is revealed in
hope and never all at once. Even on the human level, mystery

surrounds the reaction to the initial sign. One may rationalize it to a certain extent but the ultimate answer always escapes us. There is inevitably an element of blind trust, or faith. We should expect, therefore, to discover the same basic structure in the creator's dealings with his creatures. In this case, however, the problem is complicated by the fact that the offer of friendship is made indirectly. Everything hinges on the credibility of the intermediary. Paul was intensely conscious of this, and one has the strong impression that he would agree with those who blame Christians for the death or absence of God. It is not so much that Christians, through an exaggerated interest in conceptualization, have created a false image of God, but that they have imagined they could convey God's invitation to personal presence by words alone.

For Paul the reiteration of the invitation must take the form of a re-presentation. As the original invitation (Christ) was living and personal, so must be its repetition. Words are indispensable, but their sole function is clarification. They are meaningless unless they are in response to the questions generated by the contact of two personalities. Divorced from the context of the whole Christ, they only serve to mystify. The true sense of mystery can only be engendered by an element of transcendence in the believing community, an "otherness" in the bearing of its members. Unless believers are so transformed by the spirit of Christ (Rom. 8, 9-10) that the word "Father" comes naturally to their lips from something deep within them,[14] and that they in consequence live as other Christs and so constitute the whole

---

[14] The allusion is to Galatians 4, 6 and Romans 8, 15. In both of these texts the *fact* of sonship is presupposed. Paul's concern is to awaken his readers to a *conscious awareness* that they are children of God, and his argument might be paraphrased thus: "If 'Abba!' comes so naturally to your lips, impelled by something deep within yourselves, it can only be because you have *experienced* God's solicitude." R. Haughton has very acutely observed that "to call God 'Father' is not to acclaim his qualities but to bear witness to the experience of a relationship": *The Transformation of Man: A Study of Conversion and Community* (London, 1967), p. 190.

Christ, God's invitation to friendship is not a credible option. The offer can be nullified by those who pride themselves on having accepted it. In a word, the personal presence of God in the world depends on the fragile ambiguous sign he has chosen, the Church. Only when men respond to this sign can they see the hand of God in events and in material reality, and in their response the world is transformed.

Thomas Worden/*Upholland, England*

# Lord, to Whom Shall We Go?

The story is told by one of the American "death of God" theologians of how his young son returned from school one winter evening with an assignment in astronomy. He was to plot the night sky. Father and son went out together to examine the stars. The father gazed in awe at the sky, filled with wonder, and perhaps, in spite of himself, recalling the familiar words: "I look up at your heavens, made by your fingers, and the moon and stars you set in place" (Ps. 8, 3). But his meditation was soon interrupted. "Gee, Dad," shouted his son, "which ones did we put up there?"

For the younger generation the heavens do not so easily declare the glory of God, nor the vault of heaven proclaim his handiwork (cf. Ps. 19, 1). Rather they declare the glory of man and proclaim man's handiwork. They tell of the Apollos and the Sputniks, the orbits around earth and moon, the satellites and man's conquest of space, and they hold promise of still greater achievements already within man's grasp. "Look up at the skies, look at them well; and see how high the clouds are above you" (Jb. 35, 5). But to what end? To realize that God is the "Most High"? Is it not rather to realize that man is no earthbound creature but the lord of the universe? It is no longer so easy to confess that "by the Word of the Lord the heavens were made, the whole array by the breath of his mouth" (Ps. 33, 6). Surely man is well on the way to finding a less mysterious explanation of how the universe came to be than "the Lord".

The rapidity of the progress being made in science and technology is fostering the new myth of omnipotent man. It is perfectly true that the vast majority of us have very little understanding of this progress. Relatively few men are scientists; relatively few can understand the complexities of the discoveries and their application but clearly *they* do. I may understand nothing about space travel, but *they* do. I may be open-mouthed in astonishment to watch television pictures of the recovery of Apollo IX, transmitted "live" from the other side of the world, but obviously it is no mystery to *them*. I may read of computers that can do the most fantastic calculations with incredible speed, of nuclear warheads that can destroy vast areas of the earth, of new hearts substituted for old ones and human life in a test tube. The more I hear, the less I understand, except to realize with increasing awe how wonderful *they* are. And *they* are men like myself. Have men become like gods? The myth of omnipotent man exercises a powerful fascination on the minds of our contemporaries, and many are desperately trying to convince themselves that man has now acquired the knowledge of good and evil.

But the scientists whose achievements provide the stimulus for the myth makers are not as sure about this. Dr. Edmund Leach, for example,[1] has no hesitation in proclaiming that man has taken over the role of God the creator, but that he has not yet assumed the role of God the legislator. "Scientists, like God, have now become mediators between culture and nature. Modern science grew out of medieval alchemy, and the alchemists were quite explicitly men who sought to do what only gods might properly do—to transform one element into another and to discover the elixir of immortal life. They pursued these revolutionary objectives in the atmosphere of a very conservative society. Official doctrine held that the order of nature had

---

[1] "When Scientists Play the Role of God," in *The Times*, November 16, 1968.

been established once and for all in the first six days of the creation, and that the proper station and destiny of every individual had been preordained by God. The alchemists, therefore, were very properly regarded as blasphemous heretics, for they were attempting to tamper with God's handiwork. But at the present time the ordinary everyday achievements of science, which we take quite for granted, are of precisely the kind that our medieval forefathers considered to be supernatural. We can fiy through the air; we can look in on events that are taking place on the other side of the earth; we can transplant organs from corpses to living bodies; we can change one element into another; we can even produce a chemical mimicry of living tissue itself."

But Dr. Leach is not so sanguine about the ability or the willingness of the scientist to play the role of God "the lawgiver who establishes the principles of the moral code . . . the judge who punishes sinners even when human law fails to do so". He is concerned because he feels that the scientist is unwilling to undertake this second divine role which he considers, not surprisingly, to be inseparable from the first. "The scientist can now play God in his role as wonder-worker, but can he—and should he —also play God as moral arbiter? If you put this question to any group of actual scientists, the great majority will answer it with an unhesitating 'No', for it is one of the most passionately held formal dogmas of modern science that research procedure should be objective and not tendentious. The scientist must seek to establish the truth for truth's sake, and not as an advocate of any particular creed. And on the face of it, this principle is self-evident: If we are to attain scientific objectivity, moral detachment is absolutely essential."

But Dr. Leach contests this so-called self-evident principle because he is convinced that it was concocted as a defense against the attacks of religious dogmatism, which throughout history has always placed obstacles in the path of scientific progress. Moreover he suggests that the scientists themselves have never fully adhered to their own principle. "In actual practice all scientists draw the line somewhere, and they usually draw it between culture and nature. Freedom from moral restraint applies only to the study of nature, not to the study of culture. Even the Nazi scientists who experimented with human beings as if they were monkeys, rats or guinea pigs would not have challenged this distinction. They merely drew their line in a different place: from their point of view the Jews were not really human, but just a part of nature." But as Dr. Leach realizes, the question of "where to draw the line" is not to be so facilely answered by distinguishing culture from nature. It is obvious that there is no easy or certain way of making any such distinction. "The moral doubts of those who helped to design the first atomic bombs have become notorious, and today there must be thousands of highly qualified scientists engaged on hundreds of different chemical and biological research projects who face similar difficulties."

It is clear to Dr. Leach that we cannot delay any longer in facing up to the final problem that man, the master of the universe, must himself solve: "In the resulting mechanistic universe all that remains of the divine will is the moral consciousness of man himself. So we must now learn to play God in a moral as well as in a creative or destructive sense. . . . We ourselves have to decide what is sin and what is virtue, and we must do so on the basis of our modern knowledge and not on the basis of traditional categories." He ends on this somber note: "Perhaps this all sounds like a pie-in-the-sky doctrine. But unless we teach those of the next generation that they can afford to be atheists only if they assume the moral responsibilities of God, the prospects for the human race are decidedly bleak."

There is an old myth, to be found on the opening pages of the Bible, which tells how God created the heavens and the earth, and how he created man in the image of himself, with the mandate to fill the earth and conquer it. But man longed to eat the forbidden fruit which was desirable for the knowledge that it could give: the knowledge of good and evil, the knowledge that God jealously reserved for himself. When man defied God and ate of this fruit, he was expelled from Eden, for "he must not be allowed to stretch his hand out next and pick from the tree of life also, and eat some and live forever". An old myth? An outdated myth? No doubt there are many who think so, Christians included. But it will be outdated only when Dr. Leach's dream comes true, and man succeeds in acquiring that knowledge of good and evil which assures him of everlasting life.

In highlighting the dilemma which faces us when man's creativity is separated from his moral responsibility, Dr. Leach has helped to remind us of both the relevance and the challenge of the creation story with which the Bible opens. His error lies in his implying that it is only now, in an age of highly developed scientific knowledge and technological skill, that man has become aware of this dilemma. However naive the story of the creation and the fall may strike the modern reader, however superficial the attitude of our contemporaries might be to mythopoeic thinking, the fact is that man has always been aware that his knowledge of good and evil depends upon his recognition of a moral arbiter superior to himself.

It is not just now, in the 20th century, that man has tried to escape this conclusion and set himself up as the supreme judge. History is full of examples. But equally history is the record of man's failure in this regard, and of the evils resulting from the attempts. Dr. Leach is not himself overly sanguine about the chances of success in history's latest phase. Many will be in no doubt about the impossibility. In other words they will recognize the truth of the Genesis story the more clearly for having been made newly aware of what it is really about: that the way in which we live, our relationship to one another and to the material world at our disposal, can only be guided and controlled by our awareness that all is the creation of the one living and moral being whom we call God. It is only when we separate, in a way that the biblical story does not, the material creation from the men who inhabit this world that we delude ourselves into thinking that man has become God.

One may concede that it becomes easier to fall into this

delusion the greater the mastery man achieves over material creation. But there is little sign of any greater mastery being achieved over the way in which, for good or evil, man exercises this power. Even the so-called primitive story showed a clear awareness of man's superiority over the rest of creation, and its author did not need the experience of today's astonishing achievements to recognize the human potentialities. But his recognition of this truth was in the context of his realization of another, more fundamental one, as recognizable for him in the experience of actual living as it is for many of us—namely that man's creativity is fatally self-destructive when he refuses to recognize that its source lies not in himself, but in the blessing of God, that it was God who said: "Be fruitful, multiply, fill the earth and conquer it."

One thing seems clear: the choice that faces us is not between faith in the God whose transcendence is so firmly maintained through the mythological language of the biblical revelation, and faith in man as he actually exists—in you or me or the rest of us—but between the old myth of God the creator and the legislator, or the new myth of man the creator and arbitrator, whose transcendence must be maintained by way of a new mythology: the myth of man come of age, dwelling in the secular city. Precisely at a time when the mythological, symbolic language of religion is being rejected as unintelligible, we are witnessing the proliferation of new mythologies which indeed have the initial advantage of drawing their symbolic terms from contemporary civilization, and can therefore be easily mistaken for non-mythological and "real" explanations of the mystery of life. As Langdon Gilkey says: "There *are* modern secular myths as well as archaic and traditional myths. Naturally they take quite different forms than have the archaic cosmogonic myths or the mythical language of the theological tradition." [2] But we should not be deceived by this latter fact. As the same author

[2] Langdon Gilkey, "Modern Myth-Making and the Possibilities of Twentieth-Century Theology," in L. Shook (ed.), *Renewal of Religious Thought* I (New York, 1968), p. 291.

explains: "There is a split or a disjunction between modern man's *intellectual* comprehension of himself and his world— which we have called the modern spirit or mind—and his more *existential* self-understanding; that in fact the terms in which he explicitly thinks about himself are different from the terms by which he actually lives. There are many evidences of this split between the secular attitude or viewpoint on the one hand and secular existence on the other, but certainly one of them is the continuation, or better, the re-creation of myths within the modern consciousness itself." [3]

Gilkey describes myth as "the fundamental self-understanding of man with regard to his origins and to his destiny; thus it conceptualizes his comprehension of the basic enigmas of his life and provides him with some ground for confidence in dealing with these enigmas; in so doing, it also provides him with the models by which to pattern his existence and to judge his behavior and that of his fellows. Myths are, then, on the most fundamental level, the way man structures his world and his own being within it. Thus they provide the foundations for all of his interactions with that world: that is, his modes of inquiring and knowledge, of art and activity, of communal relations and roles, and of personal life and death. Insofar as modern man asks questions about his origins and his destiny, about the meaning of his life and that of his history, about what it is to be human in all of its facets, and what it is to be mortal and to die, and insofar as he affirms or seeks foundations for all he does in terms of some ultimate horizon of meaning, then *these* issues will be answered in terms of mythical discourse".[4]

It is interesting to note that the modern mythologies owe much to Darwin's *The Origin of Species*. The word "evolution" has become a potent symbolic term with the multivalent significance characteristic of mythological language. The evolutionary process scientifically observed by Darwin in the sphere of biology has become the framework or chief cornerstone of

[3] *Ibid.*
[4] *Ibid.*

many modern myths which offer the answer to man's fundamental questions concerning his origins and destiny, questions no longer asked within the limited sphere of biology, but extended to the total context of man's experience.

As J. Burrow points out, the mythologizing applications of Darwinism are no longer as convincing as they were: "The concepts of evolution and natural selection no longer seem quite the magic keys to all doors that they once did. . . . Modern philosophical tools have done severe damage to attempts to reinstate evolution as the basis of ethics, while sociologists and social anthropologists have generally repudiated as too sweeping the social evolutionary schemes of their predecessors." [5] But they remain as testimony to the perennial need for a mythology to express man's self-understanding, somewhat ironically, seeing that Darwin was considered to have dealt the final blow to the mythology of the Bible. And one hesitates to conclude that the myth of evolutionary progress is quite as played out as Dr. Burrow implies. It is surely a prominent feature in the current myth-making of the sociologists, who with a Darwin-like claim to scientific method in the observation of social facts, and with too loud a protest about being "value-free", construct their view of human living and prognosticate its future in such a way that, deliberately or not, they offer the myth of social man according to which practical decisions are being made which affect the actual lives of millions.

The picture of the secular city as delineated by Harvey Cox [6] is a well-known example. He notes the facts: that in the modern North American city more and more people are virtually unknown to their neighbors; that more and more people choose (or are forced?) to be constantly on the move; that people tend to be concerned more and more not with what a thing *is*, but with what it *does*, and look for no further explanation than can be given within the limits of human history. But he is not content

[5] Charles Darwin, *The Origin of Species*, edited with an Introduction by J. Burrow (London, 1968), p. 46.
[6] *The Secular City* (London, 1965).

to note these facts; he must also proclaim that "man" is now anonymous, mobile, pragmatic and profane.

What of the men who cannot find themselves in Harvey Cox's mythological "man"? Of his secular city it might well be said that "eye has not seen, nor ear heard". It is a city without racial violence and murderous hooliganism, without divorce courts and psychiatric consulting rooms, without workers' strikes and student protests. It is a city which contrasts strangely with this description of New York by Philip Hauser, a sociologist at the University of Chicago: "What is going on in New York is simply the logical sequence of what has been building up over some time and is likely to afflict any city in the United States any time. It is the product of a chaotic society in which we have so much emphasized individualism that we have forgotten to raise our people with some conception of their obligation to society as a whole. It simply reflects what is current in American life—the attitude of how do I get mine and the hell with every-one else and the willingness to use force for the achievement of these objectives with utter disregard for what the impact may be—the right to revert to the laws of the jungle. . . . New York just happens to be first." [7]

It is perhaps unfair to use Harvey Cox as an example of the sociological myth-maker, for it does less than justice to his intention. He is not seeking to create a new myth, but to make the old one—the Christian myth—intelligible to 20th-century man. By marrying an arbitrary selection of elements from the biblical revelation, he purports to offer his contemporaries an understanding of the secular city which shows both its Christian origin and its Christian destiny, without the obscurity and unacceptability of the mythico-symbolic choice of sociological facts with an equally arbitrary language of traditional Christian revelation. It is a fascinating picture in many ways, with many salutary reminders of the difficulties which face the preacher of the Gospel in this secular age, and with many an attractive example

[7] Alan Brien, "The New York Nightmare," *Sunday Times,* April 6, 1969.

of the secular reinterpretation of the Gospel message. But it is in the end a completely unconvincing myth of man's self-understanding. It is unconvincing to the secular man because it is too one-sided a portrayal of the secular city; it is unconvincing to the Christian because it is too one-sided a portrayal of the Christian revelation.

Cox's claim is to demonstrate that the secular city emerges from the working out of the Christian revelation, but instead of interpreting the secular world in the light of Scripture, he understands Scripture in the light of his convictions regarding the secular world. Only in the last chapter of his book, and far too belatedly, does he seem to realize that his overly simple equation of "what is happening" with "what God is doing" ignores the transcendence of God with which the biblical revelation is permeated: "This biblical God's hiddenness stands at the very center of the doctrine of God. It is so commanding that Pascal was echoing its intention when he said: 'Every religion which does not affirm that God is hidden is not true.' " [8]

Cox realizes, along with so many other serious thinkers on the subject of the contemporary world—and Dr. Leach to whom we referred earlier is a good example—that the outstanding problem, the crucial problem, concerns human responsibility, and he asks the simple but vital question: "Is this responsibility something which man himself has conjured or is it *given* to him?" His answer is equally simple and straightforward, but in such strange contrast to the impression created by his book: "The biblical answer, of course, is that it is given to him. For the Bible, after mythological and metaphysical overlay has been scraped away, God is not simply a different way of talking about man. God is not man, and man can only be really '*response*-able' when he *responds*. One must be responsible *for* something *before* someone. Man, in order to be free and responsible, which means to be *man,* must answer to that which is not man." [9]

[8] *Op. cit.,* p. 258.
[9] *Op. cit.,* p. 259.

The freedom of man is one of the greatest preoccupations of contemporary thinkers—and not surprisingly, when one considers the appalling extent to which men are robbed of their freedom and exploited by their more powerful fellow men. The cry for freedom is the rallying call for all kinds of causes, for all kinds of activity. When one reflects upon the political and economic systems of both the capitalist and the communist worlds, and the degrading enslavement of the poverty-stricken so-called "third world", one is not surprised that the burning question is "How shall man be free?" even though one is surprised that political and economic slavery is not one of the facets of Cox's overly optimistic picture of the secular city. But in uniting the two words "free" and "responsible", and claiming that this is what it means to be "man", he does put his finger on the vital spot. "No freedom without responsibility" is a well-known slogan, but it is hardly surprising that its record of success is exceedingly poor. Isn't it man's perennial dilemma that experience offers its contradiction: responsibility destroys freedom? The logic of Cox's "one must be responsible *for* something *before* someone" seems obvious. Yet *who* is this "someone" to whom I must respond? And how can I be free in the face of this someone's demand upon me? Is it not in the setting of this fundamental problem that we are offered the contemporary myth of "society"?

Let us take the example of the law concerning the termination of pregnancy passed by the parliament of Great Britain in April 1968, legalizing this operation on grounds which include both the physical and mental health of the mother, and the physical, mental and social welfare of the family—grounds said to be, by a questionable use of words, the most liberal in the world. This was a so-called progressive measure, said to be demanded by "society". But many members of the medical profession do not share the opinion of "society" and are reluctant to carry out the provisions of this law. They must therefore be issued this ominous warning: "The time has come in this area when the consultants in the medical profession will have to come down from their dictatorial heights and accept an advisory and technical role. An abortion should not be conditional on moral approval from a man who professes to be a servant of society. The new generation of doctors will probably agree; it is up to society to persuade the older ones." [10] Is the message that, in order to be free, one must be responsible to "society", the good news of salvation? Is it any more intelligible? Is it any less "mythological"? Who or what is "society"? What is freedom? To be the "servant of society"? Who then is free?

Jesus, in the opinion of Paul van Buren, comes to our rescue in this dilemma, because Jesus is the very epitome of freedom: "The New Testament points to Jesus as a man singularly free for other men, and as a man whose freedom became contagious." [11] What an extraordinary reading of the gospels van Buren gives us in attempting to substantiate this statement: "Jesus of Nazareth was a singular individual. His characteristics seem to have impressed his followers so that he stands out as a remarkably free man in the records of remembered parable, saying and incident." [12] I wonder whether it is the notion of freedom which immediately leaps to the mind of readers of parable, saying and incident in the gospels? To me at least, it is nothing less than extraordinary, if not perverse, that it should be "freedom" which is chosen as *the* hallmark of Jesus. Certainly Jesus speaks with authority when he says: "But *I* say to you. . . ." But does the Sermon on the Mount immediately and principally convey Jesus' freedom?

Take another example: "Perhaps the most radical expression of this freedom is found in an incident in which Jesus forgave a sick man his sins, and then demonstrated his right to do this by healing him. One New Testament scholar has commented on this report, that Jesus even dared to act in place of God! He did not leave it to God to forgive men their sins; he did it himself." [13] Presumably van Buren implies that when Jesus says: "But that

[10] *The Guardian,* February 10, 1969.
[11] *The Secular Meaning of the Gospel* (London, 1963), p. 157.
[12] *Op. cit.,* p. 121.
[13] *Op. cit.,* p. 122.

you may know that the Son of Man has authority on earth to forgive sins. . . ." (Mk. 2, 10), he means: "That you may know that I am free", and that the crowd who, imprisoned in their mythological world view, "glorified God" should really have glorified the freedom of Jesus. What freedom? What is this freedom van Buren is talking about? Again we read: "In miracle stories he is even presented mythologically as being free from the limitation of natural forces." [14] The one example van Buren gives for this is the stilling of the storm. According to the text, Jesus says to the disciples: " 'Why are you afraid? Have you no faith?' And they were filled with awe, and said to one another, 'Who then is this, that even wind and sea obey him? ' " (Mk. 4, 41). How can any reader suppose for a moment that the answer to their question is meant to be "the man who is free"? It is not Jesus' freedom from the limitation of natural forces which astonishes his disciples, but his authority over natural forces. But judging from the previous examples, authority and freedom are synonymous.

Perhaps it is this that explains why van Buren's emphasis on freedom seems so strange. If authority and freedom are synonymous, then they spell irresponsibility. What light does the myth of man possessing full authority in complete freedom throw on the mystery of self-understanding? What pattern does it offer for our guidance? What hope does it hold out to us in our struggle toward fulfillment? It is not the myth which unfolds the truth of our predicament, but by turns the megalomania of the master and the nightmare of the slave—unless, of course, the man possessing full authority in complete freedom is God. But van Buren cannot mean this because for him it makes no sense: the very word "God" can no longer be used in this age. But if this is granted, then van Buren's well-meaning effort to "sell" Jesus under the eye-catching label of "freedom" is a case of false pretenses which hardly calls for investigation, since it will take in very few. He is laudably aware of the present preoccupation: the search for freedom: "We would emphasize, along with

[14] *Ibid.*

many modern contemporary interpretations of christology, that the Christian perspective sees the 'true nature' of man in precisely the freedom for the others which was Jesus' own. *Human being is being free for one's neighbor.*" [15] But the whole reality of Jesus' authoritative freedom stems from his relationship with God, as the gospels make abundantly clear, though one would not understand this from van Buren's selective treatment. It is hardly surprising that he ignores St. John's gospel altogether, for here Jesus Christ is supremely "unfree" of his Father: not one work, not one word is his own, for he has come not to do his own will but the will of the one who sent him. If Jesus is not the Son of God, always doing the things that please him, then his freedom is that of the arrogant egotist, making insupportable demands upon the freedom of others. If Jesus is not the Son of God, then it is hard to accept that history can provide us with no better example of the freedom-fighter for whom so many are searching at the present time. It is the Christ of the gospels whom St. Paul proclaims has set us free.

The alternatives before us are to believe in this proclamation or to reject it; it is a strange and futile exercise to rewrite the gospels in order to give us a more intelligible Jesus—intelligible, that is, in terms of current preoccupations and current searchings. It would be so much more simple and straightforward to set out our wishful-thinking with none of the outdated trappings attaching to Jesus of Nazareth. But it is precisely these seemingly outdated trappings of history that are essential to the Christian Gospel, for it proclaims that God has *actually, in historical fact,* taken action to save us from the disaster of our own self-sufficiency. Without this involvement in human history, Christianity is nothing more than one of a number of mythological world views which, as we have tried to show, man is constantly constructing in order to find a convincing explanation of himself, and an effective way of establishing order and purpose in his struggle to survive.

The history of Jesus of Nazareth is essential to Christianity,

[15] *Op. cit.,* p. 163.

because it is the *history* of Jesus Christ, the Son of God, the historical revelation of God in action. If it is nothing more than the history of a man, singularly free or singularly wise or kind or whatever, it must simply take its place alongside many other encouraging examples of human achievement provided by the history of the human race. If it is merely an historicization of how some people see the meaning and purpose of their human life, then it must take its place alongside the great myths which the human spirit has created. And man must continue, stoically, to try and save himself. But this is not good news; this is not the Christian Gospel, and the Christian Gospel is not made more intelligible and more credible by being destroyed.

The efforts of such writers as van Buren and the whole "death of God" movement bear awesome testimony to a continuing belief that the Christian Gospel *must be,* somehow, the good news of salvation. It is essentially a movement which stems from those who have been brought up in the traditional Christian faith, and who in some way cling to this faith when overwhelmed by the evidence of its unintelligibility, its unacceptability in this secular age. But it is bound to be a short-lived movement, for it can make no sense to its own next generation which will not have had its point of departure. For them a demythologized Christianity will simply be an overcumbersome alternative to any of the de-Christianized or simply non-Christian humanisms readily available. It strikes me as a kind of "middle-aged" disenchantment. The reasons for this disenchantment are formidable enough but fundamentally it stems from that weariness and failure in courage which are always so characteristic of the problem of middle age.

The criticism voiced by Alasdair MacIntyre is accurate. He has made, to my mind, the more honest choice of the only alternative, the straightforward rejection of Christianity: "The formulas of the new theology seem to me to derive both such sense and such emotional power as they have by reason of their derivation from and association with the much more substantial faith of the past. Without that derivation and association, these formulas, far from providing modern man with a faith rewritten in terms that he can understand, would be even more unintelligible than the theology they seek to correct. Thus the new theologians are in a fundamentally false position. They in fact depend upon the traditionalism which they proclaim that they discard." [16]

"This is intolerable language. How could anyone accept it?" (Jn. 6, 60). This is surely a reasonable retort, not only after listening to Christ's discourse on the bread of life, but after listening to the whole of the Christian Gospel from beginning to end. It is simply not true that this has only become "intolerable" now. It always was intolerable. No one will doubt that modern, scientific and technological man has his own peculiar difficulties. This is obvious and the consequences are all too tangibly with us, but it is arrogantly implied that "pre-secular" man could believe just about anything because he knew no nuclear physics or bio-chemistry. Pre-secular man never existed, and human gullibility is always with us, however much it may be transformed by its new disguises. Man's search for self-understanding, his propensity to look no further than his own powers and his own selfish interests, his constant oscillation between an unwarranted optimism in his own omnipotence and a despairing pessimism in his failure to achieve the fulfillment for which he craves—all this remains the same, whatever his empirical knowledge of the universe may be. He cannot avoid realizing that there is more to the reality of existence than this, in whatever terms he admits this realization, and even when he explicitly denies it. It is for this reason that it is wrong to accept the untruth, so often foisted upon us, that Christianity is no longer acceptable because of its mythological language. Man does not, and cannot, exist without some form of myth to supply that understanding of himself which goes beyond the rational perception of his intelligence and, by influencing his whole personality, supplies the stimulus and the control without which he cannot continue his day to day living.

Therefore, the way ahead for the Christian theologian does

[16] *The Listener,* February 15, 1968.

not lie along the way of a radical demythologization of the Christian revelation, but along the way of a more perceptive appreciation of the human need which dictated the form the Scriptures took and which remains the same even in the secular city. The Scriptures do not reflect a particular "world view", as is so often said, but a view of man, historically realized in the person of Jesus Christ, a view of man based on the realization of the reality and transcendence of God. The Scriptures are unavoidably couched in terms which derive from a particular "world view" precisely because the view of man they present is both real and historically realized. If this view of man is real, then it must be couched in terms which derive from *some* world view, for man is an historical being. If this view of man has been historically realized in the person of Jesus Christ, then it must be couched in terms which derive from one particular world view, including one particular part of history. Those who long for a "demythologized" Christianity must recognize that they can only in exchange learn as much about themselves, and as little, as the history of one fellow man, however distinguished, can tell them. Those who long for a "dehistoricized" Christianity— and there are many Christians who delude themselves with this kind of wishful thinking—must recognize that they can only have in exchange an ideal construct of what life *should* mean, mythologized history, or a non-historical myth, or they can have the message concerning the transcendent God whose voice we are told was heard at the baptism of Jesus, saying: "Thou art my beloved Son; with thee I am well pleased" (Mk. 1, 11).

Neither the Scriptures nor the Christian can determine the choice men make: "No one can come to me unless he is drawn by the Father who sent me" (Jn. 6, 44), but we must continue to offer authentic alternatives. And we shall fail to do this if, on the one hand, we complacently ignore the centemporary search for a non-Christian message of salvation, or, on the other, too readily concede that modern man can no longer understand the authentic Christian Gospel. The narrowness of the prevailing scientific outlook undoubtedly makes the preaching of the

Christian Gospel more difficult. But it would be an unwarranted pessimism to resign ourselves to the impossibility of broadening this outlook: a pessimism which novelists and playwrights and painters and musicians of the so-called secular city do not share. Above all it would be a pessimism incompatible with our discipleship of Christ, confessed in the words of Simon Peter: "Lord, to whom shall we go? You have the message of eternal life, and we believe; we know that you are the holy one of God" (Jn. 6, 68-69).

# PART II
## BIBLIOGRAPHICAL
## SURVEY

Frans Neirynck/*Louvain, Belgium*

# Paul's Teaching on "Christ in Us" and "We in Christ"

S ince Adolf Deissmann suggested that the reversible formula of "Christ in me—I in Christ" was the key to Paul's christological mysticism,[1] this has become a regular discussion point in Pauline studies. Time and again the expression "in Christ" was reexamined, and the conclusion was frequently the same: "It is remarkable that it is the same for St. Paul whether we say "I am in Christ" or "Christ is in me".[2] This statement was not always put forward with the necessary qualifications, and this is partly explained by the fact that Deissmann's formula, for all its simplicity, has continued to influence even critical scholars.

## The Spiritual Christ

Deissmann's starting point was the frequent use of the preposition *en* with the dative of *Christos* (*Iesous*) or *Kyrios* (164 times). This constant use, together with the fact that it is often said of persons that they are "in Christ Jesus", points to a technical term without precedent in Pauline literature. The

[1] A. Deissmann, *Die neutestamentliche Formel "In Christo Jesu"* (Marburg, 1892); *idem, Paulus. Eine kultur- und religionsgeschichtliche Skizze* (Tübingen, ²1925), pp. 107-24 and 254-58.

[2] W. Grossouw, *In Christus. Schets van een theologie van St Paulus* (Utrecht, ²1948), p. 67.

Greek Bible provides no explanation,[3] but profane Greek usage led Deissmann to the conclusion that *en* must be understood in the graphic sense (not as interchangeable with other prepositions such as *dia*), and that the person in the dative must be a living person (and therefore not the historical Christ or the "work" of Christ).[4] "In Christ" (i.e., *within* Christ) is the key to Paul's thinking about communion with the living Christ, who is seen as that within which the Christian lives and all manifestations of Christian life are expressed.

And this is more than mere rhetoric. The parallel use of *en pneumati* (in the spirit) as well as the identification of *Christos* and *Pneuma* (cf. 2 Cor. 3, 17) shows that the glorified Christ is understood as a spiritual element in which the Christian finds himself. This explanation is confirmed by the complementary formula "Christ in me" (cf. Gal. 2, 20; 2 Cor. 13, 5; Rom. 8, 10; and the indwelling of the Spirit). Just as we say that the air we breathe is in us and fills us, and at the same time that we live in this air and breathe it, so Christ's spiritual mode of existence makes it possible for us to say "Christ in me" and "I in Christ". The two formulas present the same picture, the one seen from the point of view of Christ, the other from that of man. Later on this formula was taken over and expanded by John the Evangelist, who puts it into the mouth of the Christ of the Gospel: "Remain in me and I remain in you" (Jn. 15, 2-7, and elsewhere).[5]

## *The Personal Christ*

This article does not intend to give a survey of the authors who followed Deissmann. It is true that not each one was prepared to understand the expression "in Christ" in every instance and without exception in this mystical sense. Some objected to the expansion of the genitive construction (the so-called

---

[3] Later (*Paulus,* p. 116) he saw a hint of this in the mystical usage of "in God" and "in the Lord" in the Septuagint.

[4] His whole thesis starts from the question how a Greek-speaking reader would understand this *en* (*Die neutest. Formel,* p. 79).

[5] *Die neutest. Formel,* pp. 130-31.

*genetivus mysticus*),[6] but the main thesis of Paul's christological mysticism was accepted.[7] Two recent studies on the "in
Christ" phrase have surveyed the exegesis of this expression
since Deissmann. Both Fritz Neugebauer [8] and Michel Bouttier [9]
refer, not uncritically, to the enthusiastic reception of the "mystical explanation" in Catholic circles.[10] It might therefore be
useful to give the reaction of such scholars as Alfred Wikenhauser and Lucien Cerfaux.

In the first edition of his study of christological mysticism in
1928,[11] Wikenhauser pointed out that this topic, very popular
among Protestant authors, had received little attention from
Catholics. His work was the first extensive confrontation with
Deissmann's thesis and dealt also with the more recent literature about Paul's mysticism (expanded in the second edition of
1956). Wikenhauser agreed with Deissmann on many points.
He, too, started from the Christian's being in Christ and Christ's
being (or dwelling) in the Christian as the two aspects of the
mysterious bond uniting the two. Christ is the element in which
the Christian lives, and he uses the comparison with the fish in
the water so that the preposition *en* must be understood in its
original graphic sense and Paul can only speak of being "in
Christ" because Christ has for him a spiritual (pneumatic) mode
of existence. We have to start with the parallel of being "in the
spirit" and the image of an existence in a spiritual (pneumatic)
element (comparison with air).[12] Man, in the past, lived in the

[6] Deissmann, *Paulus*, pp. 126-27; cf. O. Schmitz, *Die Christusgemein-
schaft des Paulus im Lichte seines Genitivgebrauchs* (Gütersloh, 1924).

[7] For the older literature, see A. Wikenhauser (note 11); Deissmann,
*Paulus* p. 111, n. 1; A. Oepke, art. *"en,"* in *Theol Wört. N.T.* 2 (1935),
p. 534.

[8] F. Neugebauer, *Im Christus. En Xristoi. Eine Untersuchung zum
Paulinischen Glaubensverständnis* (Göttingen, 1961); *idem*, "Das Paulinische 'in Christo'," in *New Test. Studies* 4 (1957-58), pp. 124-38.

[9] M. Bouttier, *En Christ. Etude d'exégèse et de théologie pauliniennes.*
(Paris, 1962).

[10] See *In Christus*, p. 25; *En Christ*, pp. 8-10.

[11] A. Wikenhauser, *Die Christusmystik des Apostels Paulus* (Freiburg
i.Br., ²1956).

[12] The second edition contains a number of corrections which have increased the consistency in the author's thesis. There is no more talk of

"atmosphere" or "element" of sin, flesh, world and death, but now lives in a new "element", in Christ.

It is true that the expression "in Christ" cannot be interpreted in the mystical sense every time it is used. Under the influence of the Greek Bible the preposition *en* is used with verbs such as "to glory" or "to hope" (in Christ), and the objective redemption by God is also described as divine action or salvation "in Christ". Occasionally the expression is formalized in a way that makes it almost identical with the adjective "Christian". But even in these cases the thought of a mystical communion with the glorified Christ is not wholly absent. And once this mystical sense of "in Christ" is recognized, the same linguistic psychological interpretation penetrates the use of the genitive where Paul speaks of Christ's love, patience and saving deeds, or of himself as Christ's prisoner. "Christ in us" occurs less frequently and did not become a "formula" to the same extent as "in Christ", but it shows clearly enough that the indwelling of Christ was a viable concept for Paul. Wikenhauser also agrees with Deissmann that "mystical" should not be interpreted exclusively in the narrow neo-Platonic sense of deification or ecstatic union with the deity. "Mystical" and "mysticism" are terms to be applied to any form of piety that is marked by a direct link with the deity, and in this wider sense one can therefore also speak of the Christ-centered mysticism of Paul.

And yet, there is a basic difference between Wikenhauser and Deissmann. Wikenhauser points out that, for Paul, the spirit is not a material substance, some ethereal fluid, but the divine power (and therefore not impersonal) which intervenes in man's life and transforms it. The sphere of Christ is not spatial, but personal: to be in Christ means to be under the influence and the power of Christ as a person. Paul always thinks of Christ as a person, crucified, and glorified by God. This mysticism, centered on Christ, is more than a matter of human experience

---

the "pneuma-element", "in the Spirit" is no longer identical with "in Christ" but each formula is examined in its own right, and it is made clear that Paul's thought here is not spatial but dynamic (pp. 28, 30, 56).

or consciousness; it is an objective state that becomes real in the sacrament of baptism, and is a union of being and life with the spiritual Christ. Along with this objective divine aspect this mysticism also has a subjective human aspect which lies in religious and ethical practice. The Christian becomes a mystic in the full sense of the word only when his union with Christ reaches a special degree of intimacy.

Cerfaux has dealt with the question of Paul's mysticism in all that he has written about the Church, Christ and the Christian in the theology of St. Paul.[13] Deissmann and Wikenhauser were always mentioned, but only in his third study did he really tackle Wikenhauser's ideas (1962). Cerfaux completely agrees with him that baptism "creates a real existential bond between Christ and the Christian". He speaks of an ontological mysticism but would prefer not to use the term "mysticism" for this "supernatural" reality of Christian life, and would rather reserve it for the strictly mystical experiences which Paul knew better than most. While Wikenhauser objected to the theory of the "Christ-substance" but in fact (and not without a degree of contradiction) accepted Deissmann's literary starting point, Cerfaux has always remained skeptical on this point. He went back to the "empirical" approach, prevalent before Deissmann. Paul uses the preposition *en* to describe all kinds of relationships which get their meaning from the context and not the so-called original graphic sense of the preposition (in itself already improbable in an abstract theological language).[14] It is Paul's intense consciousness of the new reality of the Christian's existence that should explain why he constantly mentions the new and specific features of this reality in terms that are terse but by no means univocal (*raccourcis métonymiques*). "To put on

[13] L. Cerfaux, *La Théologie del'Eglise suivant saint Paul* (Paris, ³1965), pp. 179-94; *Le Christ dans la théologie de saint Paul* (Paris, 1951), pp. 243-55; *Le Chrétien dans la théologie paulinienne* (Paris, 1962), pp. 324-42.

[14] Cerfaux obviously approved (*Le Christ*, p. 247) of F. Büchsel's " 'In Christus' bei Paulus," in *Zeitschr. neutest. Wiss.* 42 (1949), pp. 141-58, where *en* not taken in the graphic sense, but as instrumental, modal or causal according to the context.

Christ" and "to be or to live in Christ" are vague and rare expressions, the content of which must be derived from the context. In any case, none of these phrases can deprive the terms *Christos* or *Kyrios* of the meaning they always have for Paul— namely, the personal Christ.

If we try to characterize Catholic exegesis of Paul's mysticism in some general terms, we may say that it does not limit this mysticism to personal experience but rather situates it at the level of "objectivity", and therefore rejects any tension between sacrament and mysticism.[15] Nor is there any tension between a mysticism centered on Christ and one centered on God. What has been said by many different authors beyond this [16] has been methodically dealt with for the first time by Wilhelm Thüsing in a monograph devoted to christocentrism and theocentrism in the epistles of St. Paul.[17]

### *"In the Spirit"*

The identification of Spirit and Christ plays an important part in Deissmann's explanation. He holds that the phrase "in the Spirit" (used 19 times) is but a variant of the phrase "in Christ". He quotes fifteen cases where "in the Spirit" occurs in connection with ideas that are linked elsewhere with "in Christ": faith (1 Cor. 12, 9), justice (Rom. 14, 7), to be justified (1 Cor. 6, 11), to be (in the meaningful sense: Rom. 8, 9), to stand firm (Phil. 1, 27), joy (Rom. 14, 17), charismata (1 Cor. 1, 8), love (Col. 1, 8), peace (Rom. 14, 17), sanctified (Rom. 15, 16; cf. 1 Cor. 6, 11), to be marked with the seal (Eph. 4, 30), circumcision (Rom. 2, 29), to witness (Rom. 9, 11), to speak (1 Cor. 12, 13), temple (Eph. 2, 22), to walk (with dative: Gal 5, 16), to be filled with (Eph. 5, 18), one body (1 Cor. 12, 13). Moreover, the expressions are used indis-

---

[15] Cf. R. Schnackenburg, *Das Heilsgeschehen bei der Taufe nach dem Apostel Paulus* (Munich, 1950), pp. 175-85.

[16] E.g. L. Cerfaux, *Le Chrétien*, p. 341.

[17] W. Thusing, *Per Christum in Deum. Studien zum verhältnis von Christozentrik und Theozentrik in den paulinischen Hauptbriefen* (Münster, 1965).

criminately side by side (Rom. 9, 1; Eph. 2, 21-22). "In the flesh" as opposed to "in the spirit" is opposed to "in Christ" (Phil. 3, 3; Philem. 16), and "in the spirit" also has a complementary formula which can be compared with "Christ in me" (Rom. 8, 3; 1 Cor. 3, 11; 6, 19).[18] A disciple of Deissmann's, Adolf Schettler, pursued this line. He explained the formula "through Christ" as expressing the spiritual influence of the heavenly Christ, and identifies the expression "through the Spirit" (Rom. 5, 5; 8, 11; 15, 30; 1 Cor. 2, 10; 12, 8) with it.[19]

This parallel between Christ and the Spirit is without doubt a key theme in the theology of St. Paul. Christology and pneumatology are closely connected, but one cannot conclude to identification merely on the ground of the formula "in the spirit". First of all, there is the question of how far we can speak here of a fixed formula. Compared with "in Christ", the frequency of its occurrence—respectively 164 and 19 times, points to a more limited application. Moreover, the variants are interesting: seven times "in the spirit",[20] six times "in the Holy Spirit",[21] four times "in [the] one spirit",[22] and once each "in the same Spirit"[23] "in the Spirit of God",[24] "in the spirit of our God",[25] and "the holy Spirit of God in whom, etc."[26]

Let us examine "in [the] one spirit". In Philippians 1, 27 the context seems to point to a purely anthropological interpretation: "to stand firm in one spirit" or "one in mind" (en heni pneumati) is followed by "one in soul (psychè)" or "unanimous". When Philippians 4, 1 speaks of "standing firm in the Lord", the meaning is less that of unity or unanimity in the fight than perseverance in loyalty and obedience to the

[18] Die neutest. Formel, pp. 85-87.
[19] A. Schettler, Die paulinische Formel "Durch Christus" (Tübingen, 1907).
[20] Rom. 2, 29; 8, 9; Eph. 2, 22; 3, 5; 5, 18; Col. 1, 8; 1 Tim. 3, 16.
[21] Rom. 9, 1; 14, 17; 15, 16; 1 Cor. 12, 3b; 2 Cor. 6, 6; 1 Thess. 1, 5.
[22] 1 Cor. 12, 9b; 12, 13; Eph. 2, 18; Phil. 1, 27.
[23] 1 Cor. 12, 9a.
[24] 1 Cor. 12, 3a.
[25] 1 Cor. 6, 11.
[26] Eph. 4, 30.

Lord (cf. 1 Thess. 3, 8; 1 Cor. 16, 13: "in the faith"). We also meet "in the one Spirit" in the passage about the distribution of the charismata (1 Cor. 12, 9). The expressions "through the spirit" (v. 8a), "in virtue of the same spirit" (v. 8b), "in the same spirit" (v. 9a), and "in the one spirit" (v. 9b) show that the charismata are attributed to the operation of one and the same Spirit, clearly understood as a person (v. 11), and for this attribution the prepositions *dia, kata* and *en* are used, in a way that makes it diffiicult to distinguish different meanings. And elsewhere we meet again "in *one* spirit" (v. 13), a phrase corresponding here to the "one body", as in Ephesians 2, 18 (cf. v. 16).

We shall have to return to the parallel references to Christ and the Spirit,[27] but from the previous quotations we can already deduce that the charismata are understood as the manifestation of the Spirit (1 Cor. 12, 7). The phenomena which accompany preaching seem also to be attributed to the working of the Spirit (1 Thess. 1, 5; cf. 1 Cor. 2, 4). For the rest, the contrast between flesh and spirit and also letter versus spirit plays an important part in Romans 2, 29 and 8, 9. Here "in the spirit" is used to indicate the Christian dispensation.[28]

### "In the Lord"

Neugebauer's recent study must be credited with having clarified the distinction between "in Christ" and "in the Lord". This distinction had already been mentioned by Werner Foerster (1924): " 'Christos' refers to the salvation and life of the faithful,

[27] Although Deissmann's list was not taken over uncritically, all authors underline the parallelism; cf. Wikenhauser, *Christusmystik*, p. 50 (cf. p. 30); L. Cerfaux, *Le Christ*, pp. 218 and 220.

[28] Thus one can speak of the "sphere" of the spirit and the "sphere" of salvation. "In Christ" then refers rather to the objective state of salvation, and "in the spirit" to the ethical conduct of the Christians. This was suggested by E. Percy, *Der Leib Christi (Soma Christou) in den paulinischen Homologoumena und Antilegomena* (Lund, 1942), pp. 18-22. Many authors have made use of it: A. Wikenhauser, *Christusmystik*, p. 30; M. Bouttier, *En Christ*, pp. 61-69; F. Gerritzen, "Le sens et l'origine de l'en Christoi paulinien," in *Studiorum Paulinorum Congressus Internationalis Catholicus 1961* (Rome, 1963), pp. 323-31, esp. p. 328.

while 'Kyrios' indicates authority and is used in connection with man's conduct, 'putting the new life into practice'." [29] Werner Schmauch (1935) was also aware of the distinction in his own way.[30] Neugebauer puts it tersely: "in Christ" and "in the Lord" are related to each other as an indicative to an imperative.[31] He limits "in the Lord" to the field of ethics, the conduct of man as creature: the human person as man and woman, in his relations with his fellow men, the man who works, writes letters, receives guests, finds joy, etc.[32]

It has rightly been observed that it does not seem right to speak of natural activity ("as creature") as if activity "in the Lord" did not manifest a new reality. Nor is it possible to separate the two formulas so radically that no overlapping can take place. The use of the two phrases is somewhat promiscuous, and we should above all realize that "in Christ" does not have the kind of limitation that is apparent in the use of "in the Lord".[33] It is in any case instructive to see how the two phrases are distributed over the theological and exhortatory passages where they occur. According to Kramer, in the theological passages, "in Christ" occurs sixteen times and "in the Lord" not at all, while in the exhortatory passages "in Christ" occurs twice and "in the Lord" seven times, The last figure could still be increased by five passages which deal with concrete questions, even though they are not exhortatory.[34] Exhortations to joy,

[29] W. Foerster, *Herr ist Jesus* (Gütersloh, 1924).

[30] W. Schmauch, *In Christus. Eine Untersuchung zur Sprache und Theologie des Paulus* (Gütersloh, 1935). Following his master, Lohmeyer he explains the formula as opposed to *en nomoi* (in the law), and distinguishes between "in Christ Jesus," "in Christ" and "in the Lord."

[31] *In Christus*, pp. 130-49, esp. p. 149.

[32] *In Christus*, pp. 133-34.

[33] Cf. M. Bouttier, *En Christ*, pp. 54-61: "in the Lord" (with nothing else), 41 times; with "Jesus" added to it, in 1 Thess. 4, 1; Rom. 14, 14; Phil. 2, 19 and Eph. 2, 19; with the addition of "Jesus Christ" in 1 Thess. 1, 1; 2 Thess. 1, 1, which makes a total of 48 times or about one-third the number of "in Christ" and its concomitants.

[34] W. Kramer, *Christos Kyrios Gottessohn. Untersuchungen zu Gebrauch und Bedeutung der christologischen Bezeichnungen bei Paulus und den vorpaulinischen Gemeinden* (Zurich/Stuttgart, 1963), pp. 176-79 (cf. pp. 140 and 176).

unanimity, constancy, strength and hospitality use "in the Lord" with the imperative. The exhortation itself is "in the Lord" (1 Thess. 4, 1; 2 Thess. 3, 12; Eph. 4, 17). Preaching and missionary work (1 Cor. 9, 12), with its successes (2 Cor. 2, 12) and toil (1 Cor. 15, 58; Rom. 12, 12) are all "in the Lord". So are the services in the community (1 Cor. 5, 12; Col. 4, 17) and the domestic duties and the greeting formulas used among Christians.[85] The title *Kyrios* indicates the glorified Christ and his dominion over the Christians, in his actual relationship with the community as with the individual. He is the authority behind apostolic leadership, and it is he who determines the whole Christian way of life in practice.

### *"Christ in Us"*

First of all, this so-called "corresponding" formula occurs only rarely, and nowhere in that direct inversion which one sometimes expects from Paul through a certain familiarity with formulas that belong to John. Moreover, the few texts usually brought up for a mystical interpretation (Rom. 8, 10; 2 Cor. 13, 5; Gal. 2, 20; 4, 19; Eph. 3, 17; Col. 1, 27) do not have the same meaning. Three texts are in the second person plural: Christ in you (en *humin*). Paul addresses the community and the phrase has an ecclesial slant (among you).[36]

Galatians 4, 19: "My children! I must go through the pain of giving birth to you all over again, until Christ is formed in you." Here Paul does not refer to Christ's indwelling in the hearts of the individual Christian but the life of the Christian Churches which he has founded in Galatia (and he uses the metaphor of the mother as well as of the father) and which it seems he must found again under the threat of false doctrine and apostasy.

---

[85] To be convinced, trust, hope "in the Lord" (Rom. 14, 14; 2 Thess. 3, 4; Gal. 5, 10; Phil. 2, 24; 2, 13): perhaps influenced by the Septuagint; already mentioned in H. Böhlig, *En Kurioi. Neutestamentliche Studien Georg Heinrici dargebracht* (Leipzig, 1914), pp. 170-75 (on the lines of Deissmann and W. Bousset).

[36] Cf. M. Bouttier, *En Christ*, pp. 80-82.

2 Corinthians 13, 5: "You can test yourselves that Jesus Christ is really in you." This is Paul's reply to those Corinthians who want to have proof that Christ speaks through Paul: Test yourselves whether you are in the faith. In 12, 20 he summed up what he was afraid of finding in Corinth: wrangling, jealousy, tempers roused, etc. Here, too, the ecclesial slant (among you) is preferable.

Colossians 1, 27: "This mystery to the pagans is Christ among you, your hope of glory." Does this make the spiritual indwelling in the Christians a prospect of future glory? The context rather suggests that Paul refers to the conversion of the pagans through which God's saving plan will be fulfilled: Christ has been brought to them through preaching.

Another text is in the first person singular. It seems obvious that Paul speaks there of his personal experience. We refer here to the well-known phrase of Galatians 2, 20: "Christ lives in me." But here, too, the phrase must be read in the context of the whole epistle. Verses 15-17 deal with the theme that "a man is righteous not through obedience to the law but through faith in Jesus Christ", and it is put in the plural. When, in the course of the argument, he passes over to the "I" formula, this "I" is impersonal, or, rather, suprapersonal: what follows applies to every Christian. I quote: "In other words, through the law I am dead to the law, so that now I can live for God. I have been crucified with Christ, and I live now not with my own life but with the life of Christ who lives in me. The life I now live in this body I live in faith: faith in the Son of God who loved me and who sacrificed himself for my sake" (vv. 19-20). The language is more that of theological argument than of mystical experience. And so Paul concludes: "If the law can justify us, there is no point in the death of Christ" (v. 21). Christ is always the personal Christ, and the Christian, too, does not lose his personality: he is justified through the faith and he lives in the faith in Christ, a life for God, Christ's life in him. The working out of and union with Christ's death and resurrection can be read in the light of Romans 6, but we shall perhaps remain closer to Paul's thought if we do not yet explicitate his meaning here in the sense of the spiritual communion with Christ in the sacrament of baptism.

Much more explicit is the text of Romans 8, 9-11: "Your interests, however, are not in the unspiritual, but in the spiritual, since the Spirit of God has made his home in you. In fact, unless you possessed the Spirit of Christ you would not belong to him. Though your body may be dead, it is because of sin, but if Christ is in you, then your spirit is life itself because you have been justified; and if the Spirit of him who raised Jesus from the dead is living in you, then he who raised Jesus from the dead will give life to your own mortal bodies through his Spirit living in you." The idea that "the spirit of God dwells in you" is repeated three times (vv. 9a, 11a, 11b), and this indwelling means justification and life. To have the Spirit of Christ and "Christ is in you" are synonymous. The same parallel occurs in Ephesians 3, 16-17: "May he give you the power through his Spirit for your hidden self to grow strong, so that Christ may live in your hearts through faith." The indwelling of Christ is linked with that of the Spirit. He is called the Spirit of Christ, but he remains the Spirit of God. The "pneuma" (spirit) is rightly seen as the key to Paul's theology. The Spirit links man with Christ, and in Christ the Spirit is the bond with God. "God has sent the Spirit of his Son into our hearts, the Spirit that cries 'Abba, Father' " (Gal. 4, 6).[37]

### "In Christ"

There is no room here for a detailed study of the phrase "in Christ". One would expect that a distinction has to be made here between Ephesians and Colossians on the one hand, and the great epistles on the other. It seems indeed that this phrase has almost become a liturgical phrase in some passages of Ephesians. But I agree with Ernst Percy who considers the ideas contained in

[37] For further development I refer again to Thüsing's work, mentioned in note 17, pp. 151-63.

the phrase the most striking point of agreement with the so-called authentic letters.[38] John Allan has maintained that in Ephesians the phrase "in Christ" has become the expression for God's activity through Christ.[39] One may wonder whether this is not also the primary meaning of the phrase in the great epistles, and thus Percy's statement would remain valid.

For Neugebauer the preposition *en* indicates an adverbial determination of circumstance, the circumstance of time: determined by. In such an "historical" view the meaning is fixed by the name that follows the preposition. I have already mentioned the distinction between *Kyrios* and *Christos.* Neugebauer groups the various uses of the phrase as follows: in connection with salvation, with the *ekklesia,* and with the apostles.[40] Kramer rightly objects that the last one constitutes only a fictitious unit, because although it refers a few times to the apostle and his work, the fact is that he is also the one who wrote the letters.[41] But Kramer agrees that Neugebauer's description, "determined by the circumstance that Jesus Christ has died and is risen again", fits the meaning of the phrase where God is shown as active. The gift of salvation or the nature of this gift is then characterized by "in Christ Jesus". The christological name "Christos (Jesus)" and God presented as active give the phrase a structural affinity with the oldest credal formula: God has raised him from the dead.

Bouttier looked for a contact in the creed: Jesus Christ is the Lord. "In the Lord" was perhaps the oldest form, and from an ecclesiological application in 1 Thessalonians, the application became soteriological, a usage which reached its peak in the christological texts of Galatians and Romans.

Elsewhere, I hope to study this phrase more in detail. Here

[38] E. Percy, *Die Probleme der Kolosser- und Epheserbriefe* (Lund, 1946), p. 231; see there also "Das *en Christoi* im Epheserbrief und in der nachpaulinischen Literatur," pp. 288-98.

[39] J. Allan, "The 'In Christ' formula in Ephesians," in *New Test. Studies* 5 (1958/9), pp. 54-62.

[40] *In Christus,* pp. 65-130.

[41] *Christos,* pp. 133-44.

I only wish to say in conclusion that more and more modern authors speak of the phrase as a "kind of formula", and pay attention to the titles *Christos* (*Iesous*) and *Kyrios* instead of being guided by a fixed meaning of the preposition. They prefer, therefore, to accept a greater variety of meaning based on the context in each case. This increases the importance of the instrumental sense, and thus comes closer to the original intent of the christological meaning.

# PART III
## DOCUMENTATION
## CONCILIUM

**Office** of the Executive Secretary
*Nijmegen, Netherlands*

Concilium General Secretariat/*Nijmegen, Netherlands*

# Is Scripture Becoming Less Important?

The question stated in the title of this article seems to suggest a hypothesis. One can point to a number of facts in all Churches which seem to indicate that the place of Scripture in the activities of these Churches is undergoing a change. This need not necessarily mean that Scripture is becoming less important, but the first impression an outsider gets is that there is a decrease in the importance attached to it. He cannot fail to see, for example, that other problems, such as *aggiornamento* and aid for developing countries, occupy far more space in world assemblies of the Churches than Scripture. This is clearly the case in Catholicism since Vatican Council II[1] and in the Protestant Churches since Uppsala.[2]

---

[1] The text of the *Constitution on Divine Revelation* and the story of how this text reached its final stage give evidence of the enthusiasm which accompanied the rediscovery and fresh appreciation of Scripture in the Catholic Church. Cf. J. Ratzinger's commentary in *Lex. f. Theol. u. Kirche* II "Das Zweite Vatikanische Konzil" (Freiburg/Basle/Vienna, 1967), pp. 498-503, 570-81). Several encyclicals, such as *Populorum Progressio* and *Pacem in Terris,* have put the accent on the problems of the Church and the world today. Even *Humanae Vitae* abandoned the attempt to argue from Scripture.

[2] W. A. Visser 't Hooft drew attention to this fact in his address "The Mandate of the Ecumenical Movement" to the World Council of Churches (1968) at Uppsala. See also R. Dickenson, *Richtschnur und Waage. Die Kirchen und die sozialökonomische Entwicklung* (Geneva, 1968), pp. 51-57.

What these changes will ultimately lead to is hard to say. Therefore, it seemed useful to gather some of the facts that clearly point to a change and then to see what reasons some modern authors adduce to explain this striking phenomenon. After this we can see whether it is possible to produce a provisional assessment of the situation. It is obvious that these facts did not emerge in all countries at the same time or with the same urgency. Interest in Scripture, for instance, was alive in German-speaking countries before it was aroused in Latin America. But it is true that the facts all seem to converge and to develop the same tendency.

# I

## THE FACTS

The first fact that strikes us is that interest in the Bible reached a peak and then suddenly seemed to diminish. Since Vatican Council II and Uppsala the interest in the function of Scripture for the spiritual life, theology and use in the Churches apparently lessened, while in some sects, such as the Jehovah Witnesses and some fundamentalist groups, it seemed to become even more essential.

At Uppsala F. Coggan gave a survey of the state of affairs in the bible societies. In spite of general optimism they appeared in fact to be declining. From the start [3] these societies showed a steady progress among both Protestants and Catholics. Their work was highly appreciated in the missions. Not without an element of boastfulness, regularly published statements announced that the Bible was the most translated and most read book. [4]

---

[3] The oldest bible society, the Society for Promoting Christian Knowledge, was founded in London in 1698. In 1804 the English bible societies united and formed the well-known British and Foreign Bible Society. In 1816 the American Bible Society was set up in the United States and the Scotch bible societies became the National Bible Society of Scotland. These three societies are the main ones. Cf. J. Schmid, "Bibelgesellschaften," in *Lex. f. Theol. u. Kirche* II, pp. 246-49.

[4] By way of illustration, the British and Foreign Bible Society has

Because this is no longer the case, one might attribute the decline to the normal situation where needs have been satisfied; however, it was observed at the same time that, with the new understanding of the Churches' missionary function,[5] the spreading of the Bible in the languages of the missionary peoples had yielded to other tasks which the Churches had come to see as more urgent, such as aid for developing countries, the fight against racial discrimination and the building of peace—all this often in union with the United Nations. In addition bible clubs, which were launched after World War I particularly in German-speaking regions, and which sprung up everywhere like mushrooms after World War II, as well as Scripture courses and popular magazines about Scripture as the source of life,[6] saw a sharp decline in their popularity.

Here again one might see an obvious explanation in the change from a reading culture to an audio-visual one in our society, a process powerfully helped along by the spread of the mass media. This shift undoubtedly influenced the factual decrease in Scripture reading. It is, however, not the only reason since, for instance, the interest in films about the Bible which translated the "greatest story ever told" in visual terms for the mass media, often without much feeling for the real religious

---

published more than half a million Bibles or parts of Bibles. In 1956 the United Bible Societies distributed 26,379,142 Bibles. In the 19th century there were 494 translations of the Bible, and 560 other translations had been added by 1950. Cf. J. Schmid, *loc. cit.*, and B. Hemelsoet and H. Haag, "Bibelübersetzung(en)," in *Bibel Lexikon* (Einsiedeln/Zürich/Cologne, ²1962), pp. 239-45.

[5] Cf. the *Decree on the Church's Missionary Activity,* the *Constitution on the Church in the Modern World,* and the encyclicals mentioned above. A major change also took place in the World Council of Churches between Edinburgh (1910) and Uppsala (1968): the mission is understood in a new sense and internal ecclesiastical problems are no longer solved by having recourse to Scripture, but on the basis of the Churches' responsibility for the Church and with the help of sociological data. Cf. *Von Neu-Delhi nach Uppsala 1961-1968* (Geneva, 1968).

[6] Cf. "Bibelbewegung," in *Bibel-Lexicon* (Einsideln/Zürich/Cologne), pp. 210-12; J. Kürzinger, "Bibelbewegung," in *Lex. f. Theol. u. Kirche* II, pp. 344-46; see also the vindication of the new formula in *Bible et Vie Chrétienne* 84 (1968).

content of this story, declined in a way which alarmed the film producers (cf. the failure of Pasolini's film). The liturgical renewal, inaugurated by Guardini,[7] from the beginning ran parallel with the renewed interest in the Bible. A systematic reading of the Bible was linked with the celebration of the liturgy,[8] but in the liturgical experiments today one notices a tendency to replace Scripture reading by other matter, or at least to mix the two. This looks like a practical admission of the fact that Scripture can be replaced, and is an illustration of the phenomenon that important Christian denominations are allowing themselves to be guided more and more by factors other than Scripture. The business of the Churches is not determined by urgent events that take place in our society. In theology, too, where the concrete situation with its actual problems has become a *locus theologicus,* the importance of Scripture texts for proof diminished almost "naturally".

Insofar as Protestant theology is concerned, Pannenberg mentioned this tendency when he stated that theology has not remained faithful to its proper object, the universal God as creator of all, and allowed itself to be limited to the God of revelation.[9] This limitation has taken place in Protestant theology more or less as a matter of course. Theology began to see itself as the positive science of revelation. And here Pannenberg observes that this position seems to become increasingly untenable because of the way in which Scripture itself has come to be subject to the criticism of the historical sciences. A recent controversy between Rahner and Lohfink [10] about the place of

[7] Cf. E. Tewes, "Romano Guardini," in *Liturgisches Jahrbuch* 19 (1969), pp. 129-41.

[8] L. Grollenberg, for instance, maintains that the Bible only comes really to life in the communal celebration. Cf. "Het 'begeleidend schrijven.' Bij het debat over de zin van het Oude Testament," in *Tijdschr. v. Theol.* (1962), pp. 347f. For an example of the mixture of scriptural and literary readings, see M. Tosco, *Alzo zero—provocazioni quotidiane per vincere l'isolamento in questo mondo tutto da rifare* (Turin, 1968).

[9] W. Pannenberg, "Die Krise des Schriftprinzips," in *Grundfragen systematischer Theologie* (Göttingen, 1967), pp. 11-21.

[10] K. Rahner, "Zur Neuordnung der theologischen Studien"; N. Loh-

Scripture in theological training points in the same direction. And the discussion is not limited to a theoretical discussion about method. If, for instance, we read today an article on the place of woman in the functions of the Church or on the changing image of the priest, we see that the data mentioned in the Bible are not the only norms that decide the theological issue; it is also decided by the social factors which determine functions in society, and therefore also by the "spiritual" functions.

Something similar can be seen in the theological approach to the structures of the Church, and certainly not only among Western European authors.[11] And all these questions are not merely the concern of professionals. When well-disposed young people are asked about the importance of Scripture for their opinions and practice, one finds there a certain disillusionment with Scripture. An obvious explanation is once again that the members of the younger generation with their new mentality ask the wrong questions when they turn to Scripture. But then one touches also—even though implicitly, as is so often the case in these matters—upon one of the real reasons why Scripture seems to have lost some of its importance: too many questions are put to the Bible, and people clearly have more urgent problems to cope with than those for which Scripture cares to give a solution. Along with this one also hears reproaches such as: Scripture supports colonialism; it encourages the alienation of man because it is used as a prop to support authority or as a political instrument; [12] it is anti-feminist; it does not offer any

---

fink, "Text und Thema. Anmerkungen zum Absolutheitsanspruch der Systematik bei der Reform der theologischen Studien"; K. Rahner, "Die Exegese im Theologiestudium. Eine Antwort an N. Lohfink": all in *Stimmen der Zeit* 181 (1968), pp. 1-21; 120-26; 196-201.

[11] See, among others, I. Illich, "Métamorphose du Clergé," in *Esprit* 35 (1967), pp. 584-601; A. Greeley, "A Priest To Turn To," in *A Future To Hope In* (New York, 1969), pp. 261-76; M. Bellet, *La peur ou la foi. Une analyse du prêtre* (³1967); H. Küng, *Structures of the Church* (New York, 1964).

[12] Something similar is happening in Israel where some right-wing groups use the Bible for political ends. Cf. F. Marquandt, "Christentum und Zionismus," in *Evang. Theologie* 28 (1968), pp. 629-60.

sufficiently detailed methods to humanize life; it is too authoritarian and does not recognize the values contained in the holy books of the other great religions of mankind; it seems to be unable to provide a solution for such urgent issues as racial discrimination and is too bound up with the past to throw any light on the future.

The methods used in catechetics today do not begin by confronting the learner with the history of the Old and New Testaments. They rather start with the concrete situation in which the learner, whether child or adult, actually finds himself in order to stimulate a process of growing awareness, which will only directed toward the message of the Bible in the last stage.[13]

The less obvious the importance of something is, the more it needs to be stressed. This is why, now that the importance of Scripture seems to be on the decrease, the interested Christian is flooded with literature about its importance, authority and meaning.[14] This literature is naturally so academic that the

---

[13] Cf. H. Halbfass, *Fundamentalkatechetik* (Düsseldorf, 1968), pp. 102-09, 299-359; *Grondlijnen voor een vernieuwde schoolkatechese* (Nijmegen, 1967). Most striking is "Programma voor de Lagere Technische School," in *Verbum* 33 (1966), pp. 121-67, where the Bible is only mentioned incidentally, and the concrete method for the application of this program by P. Bakker and W. Saris, *"Ik van de anderen"* and *"Ik zelf"* (Haarlem, 1966); H. van Leeuwen, "In de wereld niet van de wereld," in *Verbum* 35 (April 1968), pp. 138-73; *idem*, "Met of zonder Bijbel?" in *School en godsdienst* 22 (Oct. 1968), pp. 274-83; both of these articles deal with the use of the Bible in various forms of religious instruction. This problem will also be dealt with in Volume 53 of *Concilium*.

[14] No complete bibliography is possible here. For the German language, see J. Brosseder, "Autorität der Schrift und Autorität der Kirche," in *Una Sancta* 22 (1967), p. 161, note 1. Other languages: J. Baker, "The Supremacy of Scripture," in *Theology* 69 (1966), pp. 11-116; J. Coppens, "Schriftkritiek en schriftgezag in de R.K. theologie," in *De bijbel in het geding* (Nijkerk, 1968), pp. 65-83; L. Gilkey, "The Authority of the Bible. The Relation of the Bible to the Church," in *Encounter* 27 (1966), pp. 112-23; A. Grillmeier, "Die Wahrheit der hl. Schrift und ihre Erschliessung," in *Theol. u. Phil.* 41 (1966), pp. 161-87; J. Koole, "Schriftgezag en kanon," in *De bijbel in het geding* (Nijkerk, 1968); J. Sanders, "The Meaning and Authority of the New Testament," in *Soundings. Essays Concerning Christian Understanding* (Cam-

uninitiated cannot make much sense out of it. As a result, instead of reading Scripture, many have instead turned to reading scientific studies about Scripture.[15]

Although many authors do not explicitly deal with this decline in the importance of Scripture but adroitly cover it up, there are some who try to find an explanation for this decline. They rightly point out that this process is not set off by a loss of the objective importance of Scripture itself but by factors outside Scripture which are determined by the culture in which we live. Other causes are also mentioned, but incidentally. To give a brief survey of all these causes is the main point of this article. There are first of all a number of cultural factors which made the importance of Scripture relative, just as they showed the relative character of all that was presumed to be sacred or absolute. But there are also factors which are the result of a change in attitude toward such an important category for the importance of Scripture as "authority". A change in attitude toward authority in general is bound to affect the authority of Scripture. While the importance of Scripture is not the same as its authority, it is nevertheless a fact that the exceptional importance the Churches attached to Scripture was closely connected with the exceptional and absolute authority these same Churches attributed to the "book of books". Finally, there are factors inherent in Scripture itself which help us to understand this decline in its importance. For each of these three groups of reasons we shall refer to opinions taken from the most accessible literature, without pretending to be exhaustive, but aiming at a clear and coherent orientation. In the last section of this article we hope to assess the positive consequences of this decline in the importance of Scripture.

---

bridge, [2]1966), pp. 123-45; M. Schoonbrood, "L'autorité de la Bible," in *La Rev. Nouv.* 25 (1969), pp. 470-78; G. Tavard, "L'autorité de l'Ecriture et la Tradition," in *Problèmes de l'autorité* (Paris, 1962), pp. 39-59.

[15] Cf. the warning given by B. van Iersel, "Interpretatie van de schrift en van het dogma," in *Tijdschr. v. Theol.* 8 (1968), p. 314.

## II
### THE REASONS

*General Reasons*

We cannot wash our hands of this decrease in the actual importance attached to Scripture in the framework of the Churches' practical existence by saying that it is now clear that the post-war peak of interest in the Bible was simply a flash in the pan. We have here something more than a superficial freak of fashion.

In the first place there is the fact that the ordinary faithful, too, now know that "the" book is in fact a collection of very different books which all originated in different and ancient cultural periods belonging to the past.[16] Such a book will then inevitably share in the way modern culture looks at all that is past and gone. We are so fascinated by the future and so disillusioned with the past that we distrust anything, however valuable in itself, that has come to us from older cultures.[17] This holds for such classical authors as Homer and Tacitus, for the old classical university, for the classical models of democracy, and so also for the old book we call Scripture.

Then there is the general trend toward desacralization which was bound to affect the sacred character of Scripture. Why, people ask, is Scripture "the" book and not simply a valuable book among many others, the authority of which must depend on its contents? This is no longer a rhetorical question to be disposed of with an apologetic argument. Through history we

---

[16] Cf. W. Marxsen, *Das Neue Testament als Buch der Kirche* (Gütersloh, 1968), pp. 35-40; H. Schlier, "Was heisst Auslegung der Schrift?" in *Besinnung auf das Neue Testament* (Freiburg/Basle/Vienna, 1964), pp. 35-62.

[17] On this new awareness, see H. Lefebvre, *La vie quotidienne dans le monde moderne* (Paris, 1968); L. Landgrebe, "Das Zeitalter ohne Menschenbild," in *Gegenwart und Tradition* (Freiburg i. Br., 1969), p. 151.

know how Scripture came to occupy a privileged position in the process of Western civilization, apart from its formative influence. When Christianity was accepted in Western society (with the peace of Constantine) and later became a State religion, it landed in a rhetorical culture. This culture became Christian because the classical authors, who were the sources for the rhetorician, were replaced by Scripture. Until—and even during—the Middle Ages Scripture was not only "the" book, but, for many of the thinking elite, also was the only book. Chenu [18] has pointed out that this was bound to lead to an approach to Scripture as the exclusive source of truth. The intelligentsia could always find an answer in Scripture, not only for questions about truth, but also for all the political problems which reared their heads in this religious culture.

After the collapse of the Western Roman Empire Scripture had not only become the substitute for the classical authors, but also the manual for a theocratic regime, inasmuch as the political functions of emperor and king were sacralized on the ground of Scripture.[19] The Reformation and the invention of the printing press popularized these opinions, although Scripture was already clearly manipulated within the framework of other purposes than the purely religious ones—namely, political purposes and the maintenance of the fictitious world of the Renaissance popes and the one truth. In a previous issue of *Concilium,* Dussel has shown that, in spite of this use of the Bible, the autonomy of the various sciences nevertheless progressed, though slowly.[20] During the Enlightenment the petrified opposing fronts came to life again: the claims to the universal truth, on which the Churches pretended to have the monopoly,

[18] M.-D. Chenu, *Introduction à l'étude de Saint Thomas d'Aquin* (Univ. of Montréal, ²1954), pp. 106-17.

[19] Cf. Y. Congar, "The Sacralization of Western Society in the Middle Ages," in *Concilium* 47, pp. 55-71.

[20] E. Dussel, "From Secularization to Secularism," in *Concilium* 47, pp. 93-119; K. Scholder, *Ursprunge und Probleme der Bibelkritik im 17. Jahrhundert* (Munich, 1966).

were attacked by such people as Lessing.[21] Doubt was cast on the sacred character and the absolutist character of the Church's structures. With the onset of literary historical criticism Scripture was subjected to the same scientific procedures that were applied to other ancient authors and their writings. This scientific approach treated Scripture as one book among others, and this was bound to affect the sacred character of Scripture, since the better insight into the way Scripture originated, its historicity, the pluriformity of its doctrine, the origin of the canon, etc., made people more aware of the fact that Scripture had an historically conditioned past and that the understanding of it is conditioned by one's own culture.

In spite of a renewed interest in Scripture since the rise of romanticism and the school of Tübingen,[22] the sacred character of the Bible was so diminished that, when tradition was called a source of revelation apart from Scripture, the term "tradition" in fact came to cover the whole religious culture. After 1848 the Churches withdrew to their own positions over against the world and its growing autonomy, and so made Scripture share in their own isolated existence. Scripture became a book of the Churches, with the result that the decline in the prestige of the Churches automatically resulted in a decline in the prestige of Scripture because of this exaggerated identification of the Churches with Scripture. The attempts made by the Churches to link up again with modern culture (modernism, dialectical theology, demythologization, dialogue with Marxism, the positive appreciation of other religions, the *aggiornamento* of Vatican Council II) cast their shadows on the importance of Scripture which was taken for granted for too long a time.

The conviction that human reality is an historical reality has

[21] E. Hirsch, *Geschichte der neuern evangelischen Theologie im Zusammenhang mit den allgemeinen Bewegungen des europäischen Denkens* IV (Gütersloh, ³1964), pp. 157f.
[22] A. Hulst, "Schriftgezag en geschiedenis," in *Rondom het Woord* 10 (July 1968), pp. 332-45. Cf. H. Haag, "Katholische Tübinger Exegese rund um die Sündenfallerzählung," in *Theologie im Wandel* (Munich/Freiburg, 1967), pp. 333-55.

often been said to constitute the greatest change in the modern mentality. By working for the future, man realizes himself. Scripture gives us a salvation history which is separated by thousands of years from what is happening now. This also held, of course, for Augustine, Luther and Bossuet. But the need to bridge this distance has become acute because of this living awareness of modern man that he is a creature of history. Hermeneutics has been trying to fill this need, but is it possible to make our outlook and understanding and that of those who wrote the sacred books cover each other without sacrificing one side to the other?

Gadamer thinks it is possible.[23] For him Scripture is acquiring a new authentic meaning. But even then we still have the problem of how this particular history of so many centuries back can tell us something about what Pannenberg calls *Universalgeschichte* (universal history)?[24] How can the history we make still be the history made by the universal God? How indispensable can the salvation history of Scripture be for us and for this universal history without our history today losing its autonomy?

All these questions are put to the modern author. Pannenberg thinks he has a positive answer.[25] But for the believer who thinks and feels in terms of today, the true history is no longer prefigured in "the" book: real history has still to be made. And so the modern reader reads a book like the Bible differently, and the book exists as a book only insofar as it is read. The reader and his future have become more important than the book. The modern reader therefore seems to find it difficult to see in this book a definitive or pre-determined model of history, but he will be prepared to accept it as an inspiration when it appears to be relevant to his history. Rightly or wrongly,

[23] Cf. H. Gadamer, *Wahrheit und Methode* (Tübingen, [2]1965), pp. 313f.; P. Ricoeur, "Le Christianisme et le sens de l'histoire," in *Histoire et Vérité* (Paris, [2]1964), pp. 81-99.

[24] Pannenberg, *loc. cit.*, pp. 19f.

[25] *Ibid.*, pp. 17-21.

the authority of man as he is today prevails. It is in any case a factor which plays a part in the importance attached to Scripture. The text: "You have learned how it was said to our ancestors . . . but I say this to you" then seems to underscore the importance of actuality, and one is tempted to identify oneself with this "I" as an example of one's own attitude. In this context the triangular relationship of Scripture, indispensable interpreter and modern reader becomes a hindrance to the immediate relevance and importance of Scripture itself.[26] But this difficulty besets the reading of any old book and any classical author, and the Bible is no exception.

## The Crisis in Authority

The importance attached to Scripture used to depend for a large part on the absolute authority with which it was credited. Where this authority is queried, the importance of Scripture will be queried, too. Here a distinction should be made between the importance of Scripture for the faith, as the Word *about* God for Christian life, and its importance as the Word *of* God for the Churches, the institution.[27] The crisis currently besetting any kind of authority affects Scripture mainly in the second sense. The importance of Scripture in the first sense might gain by it. The changed attitude toward authority in our society might be briefly described as follows: In our society authority is no longer inherent in dignity, origin or appointment, but must prove itself through its accomplishments; it must make itself credible. The sciences, for instance, have authority not because "the master has spoken" but because they become credible through their results. Formal authority is rejected, but authority based on satisfactory exercise is accepted.[28] These opinions operate also in the appreciation of the authority of Scripture. Apart from

[26] B. van Iersel, *loc. cit.*, pp. 315f.; cf. A. Vögtle, "Historisch-objektivierende und existentiale Interpretation," in *Gegenwart und Tradition* (Freiburg i. Br., 1969), pp. 217-26.

[27] M. Schoonbrood, *loc. cit.*, pp. 474-76.

[28] J. Bochenski, *Logik der Religion* (Cologne, 1968), pp. 106-08; J. David, *Loi naturelle et autorité de l'Eglise* (Paris, 1969), pp. 84-92.

the formal assertion that God is the author of Scripture, people know painfully little about the specific author of the various books of Scripture.[29]

There is therefore an inclination to make the authority of Scripture depend on whether Scripture presents itself as credible in our age. For those of a pietistic trend, and particularly for some sects,[30] this is even the absolute norm for the authority of Scripture: a one-sided application of the old principle of Scripture's "clarity" and "self-sufficiency". This can become a subjective norm, although not necessarily so. The other extreme is to attach the authority of Scripture to the magisterium. Marié has observed that this model of authority leads us to a vicious circle: the magisterium has authority because it derives its existence from Scripture, and Scripture is binding because and insofar as the magisterium interprets it.[31]

It is remarkable to see how, since Luther, the expertise in interpreting Scripture has increased, and the importance of Scripture with it.[32] We therefore have here an authority that has arisen by proving itself. Bultmann's view that Scripture has authority if it leads me to understand myself and a meaning for my existence is in the line of that attitude to authority which seeks its strength in credibility, but the result seems too limited for a genuine authority, because it suggests that it is based on an understanding of which "I" am the principal, if not the only, object. This makes one wonder whether there is not a great deal more to understand than oneself? There is the whole present situation and the development of society. If Scripture is to be truly credible, should it not also lead to an understanding of people, the world, history and the Absolute?[33] Does reading

[29] W. Marxsen, *op. cit,*. pp. 37-39.

[30] H. Spier, *De Jehovah's getuigen en de bijbel* (Kampen, 1961); R. Pietz, "Die Autorität der H. Schrift in den Sekten der Gegenwart," in *Jahrbuch d. Evang. Bundes* III (Göttingen, 1960), pp. 110-46.

[31] R. Marié, "Foi et interprétation," in *Etudes* (May 1969), p. 674; P. Grelot, *Bible et théologie* (Paris, 1965), p. 19.

[32] Cf. *Klare Wijn. Rekenschap over geschiedenis, geheim en gezag van de Bijbel* (The Hague, 1967), pp. 24-27.

[33] Cf. van Iersel, *loc. cit.,* pp. 323-26.

Scripture not lead to an identification with the persons and patterns of life shown forth in Scripture, and does this stimulate the religious authenticity of the modern reader? On this last point the authority of Scripture will be subject to the critical judgment of psychoanalysis and ethics.[34] In a kind of anonymous way the question of authority is always present. According to Schoonbrood,[35] the silence of the theologians on this question of the changing authority of Scripture is significant, although we do not altogether agree with him here.[36]

There is still another way in which the changing attitude to authority seems to weaken the importance of Scripture. The results of historical and critical exegesis have shown up a multiplicity of doctrines in Scripture, and the authority of the one homogeneous doctrine finds itself under attack. One can no longer simply say that Scripture teaches this or that. Chenu [37] quotes a medieval author who said that the univocal doctrinal authority of Scripture is like a wax nose which can be twisted in various directions—a statement which still finds expression in the popular saying that the devil can cite Scripture.

Has Scripture then no authority at all? Indeed it has, but not in the sense of something that is objectively and universally valid. Scriptural authority is not the formal authority of a lifeless object. It must not be isolated from the life of faith which is concentrated around the living reality of Jesus.[38] Insofar as Jesus is alive and makes himself credible in the life of the community as "the way, the truth, and the life", Scripture has authority. But is that not again a vicious circle? Jesus is the authority, and both Scripture and tradition always converge on

[34] C. van Ouwerkerk, "Secularism and Christian Ethics," in *Concilium* 35 (1967), pp. 97-139.

[35] *Loc. cit.*, p. 470.

[36] See E. Schillebeeckx, "Het 'rechte geloof', zijn onzekerheden en zijn criteria," in *Tijdschr. v. Theol.* 9 (1969).

[37] M.-D. Chenu, *La Théologie au douzième siècle* (Paris, ²1966), p. 361, quotes Alain de Lille: "Auctoritas cereum habet nasum, id est, in diversum potest flecti sensum."

[38] Cf. R. Slenczka, *Geschichtlichkeit und Personsein Jesu Christi* (Göttingen, 1967), pp. 332f.; cf. J. Berten, "Christologie et recherche historique sur Jésus," in *Rev. Sc. Phil. et Théol.* (April 1969), pp. 233-44.

him. But the fact that Jesus is "the" authority we learn again from Scripture. The circle seems to be a magic circle which we cannot break through unless there is access to Jesus from elsewhere and this Jesus can make Scripture credible through the community.[39]

The problem of Jesus [40] seems to be more than an exegetical or historical question. It must also be approached by the experience of faith in the Christ of "today, yesterday and tomorrow". In any case, it is no longer possible for the modern believer with his new awareness of things to subscribe to Barth's view of the authority of the Bible as an absolute Word which cuts right across the human word so that this human word is constantly subject to the critical judgment of the former. It is significant that Barth never managed wholly to dispose of Schleiermacher, the theologian of religious experience.[41] Scriptural authority and human autonomy cannot compete. Rahner rightly says,[42] in speaking about Scripture and tradition, that, from the religious point of view, it is impossible to maintain two sources. There must be ultimately one source which is the foundation of authority, and in the Christian awareness of today that is not the formal authority of the institution but the inherent personal authority of the Lord who continues to live among his brethren in the faith and whom they confess. This element of community in faith cannot be understood in the matter of authority as a general confirmation of some individual conviction, but as the awareness, nourished by dialogue and practice, that others, too, know themselves as freely committed to this Jesus who makes himself credible. In this way scriptural authority becomes credible in Jesus and the community united with Jesus.

[39] As an illustration of the opposite, see Buber in U. Hedinger, "Bubers Kritik an Jesus," in *Theol. Zeitschr.* 25 (1969), pp. 40-56.

[40] L. Malevez, "Jésus de l'histoire, fondement de la foi," in *Nouv. Rev. Théol.* 99 (1967), pp. 785-99.

[41] Cf. B. Willems, "Barth's afgebroken gesprek met Schleiermacher," in *Tijdschr. v. Theol.* 9 (1969), pp. 2-10.

[42] K. Rahner, *Schriften zur Theologie* VI (Einsiedeln, 1965), p. 121.

That Christian experience and the Christian spiritual life play an important part here is obvious. It is equally obvious that theology on this point is still very inadequate. This can only be overcome, however, by continual ethical practice (*Nachfolge*). Otherwise, scriptural authority will continue to decline, and the Bible will become more and more just one book among others, and those whom the New Testament calls "the followers of the way" (cf. Acts 9, 2; 22, 4) will become "those who cling to the Word". In other words, scriptural authority depends on the Jesus who is present and makes himself credible in the practice of Christian life. On these lines Scripture can then again be free from the institutional Churches and break through the isolated existence that was imposed upon it by the institution. But this requires that the dialectic between the pre-war return to the sources and the post-Vatican II *aggiornamento* will grow into a genuine synthesis.

## Factors Inherent in Scripture

Some factors that have reduced Scripture to a more relative position in our time are due to the peculiar nature of Scripture. We shall not bother about such doctrinal specifications of this peculiarity as the verbal inspiration of Scripture. At present this suffers at least from the problem of unverifiability, like any other form of fundamentalism.[43] But some special inspiration continues to belong to this peculiar nature of Scripture. For example, it cannot be reduced to a poetical or religious inspiration of the kind that can be found in other books. Theology will undoubtedly make more use of the results of linguistic analysis in order to arrive at an inspiration which correlates with revelation via the analogies of this divine inspiration in other writings.[44] The content of the narratives in Scripture—e.g.,

[43] Fundamentalism is not yet dead; see J. Michael, "Fundamentalismus," in *Lex. f. Theol. u. Kirche* IV, pp. 451f. For the history of "verbal inspiration", see J. Beumer, "Die Inspiration der Heiligen Schrift," in *Handbuch der Dogmengeschichte* I (Freiburg/Basle/Vienna, 1968), p. 3b.

[44] L. Alonso Schökel, "El proceso de la inspiración: hablar y escribir," in *Biblica* 46 (1966), pp. 269-86.

their miraculous features—also makes the importance of Scripture more relative today, although this may be only a temporary and unjustified phase.[45] Then there is also the realization that Scripture speaks in the first instance to other people than us, who are living today, which makes it easier for modern man to ignore the authority which Scripture can still exercise in spite of everything. This stresses the importance of the expert interpreter and the officeholder of the future who will have to acquire this expertise which must make the Word addressed to others relevant to human beings of today.

Zahrnt,[46] who had dealt with this flight from the relevance of Scripture in the first of his contributions to the *Evangelische Kirchentag* of 1969 in Stuttgart, points out that, in connection with this problem, the Churches cannot overestimate the problem of historicity. If the Churches are suspected of spiritual weakness and lack of credibility, this is without doubt also connected to the fact that, while they may not altogether try to steer away from history, they certainly do not treat this history very seriously. To this we should add a breakdown in communications, which certainly does not make Scripture more important for the modern believer, and which results from the fact that the authorities in the Church do not really try to transmit the results of biblical exegesis to the faithful. Some Churches even create the impression that the Gospel of the biblical scholars is another Gospel than that of the Churches (*Kein anderes Evanglium*).[47]

And so the faithful remain uninformed about the true results of exegesis until they pick up this information in more tendentious and less appropriate quarters.[48] The shock that this pro-

[45] For the question of the miracles, cf. W. de Pater, "Wonder en wetenschap: een taalanalytische benadering," in Tijdschr. v. Theol. 9 (1969), pp. 11-54.

[46] H. Zahrnt, *Bijbelkritiek en geloof* (Utrecht, 1967), p. 15.

[47] Cf. the pamphlet *Kein anderes Evangelium*, published by the Bkenntnisbewegung "Kein anderes Evangelium" which belongs to the Evangelical Church of West Germany.

[48] Two examples: the articles that appeared in *Der Spiegel* 20 (1966), "Jesus und die Kirchen", and in *Paris Match* 1014 (1968), "Le grand trouble des Catholiques".

duces in the faithful then has the effect of undermining their confidence in the Churches. They will then only see the importance which the Churches attribute to Scripture and no longer that importance which is inherent in Scripture itself. One sometimes has the impression that those who should convey the meaning and message of Scripture behave like postmen who shove letters full of inspiring and encouraging messages through the letterbox and then take to their heels without further explanation.[49]

# III
## LOOKING AHEAD

Should this admittedly rather rough survey disturb us? Of course it does, but it needn't. All this has a very positive aspect. It is a clarifying and purifying process with regard to the authority of Scripture. The genuine authority will, among other things, be able to measure up to the criticism of an adult science and the broader consciousness of modern man. The liberating and effective authority of Scripture lies in that it teaches us the freedom and gives us the courage to receive the future from God, to invade and to conquer it—in other words, to receive it as an *adventus Domini,* the coming of the Lord. The authority —and, with it, the importance—of Scripture will gain according to whether we see and let others see that it is not being manipulated in favor of some particular good, not even the particular good of the Churches. We cannot go back. One cannot expect that the authority of the past will be reestablished. Probably we shall come to realize that we have often let the Gospel drop out of our hands and that it was picked up by others who are unaware of the fact that they are confessing Christ. And then we also shall be able to take it in our own hands again. Scripture was not given to the Churches to cling to as a privilege but in order to make it public property. Where Scripture lands outside

[49] J. de Jong, *Voorrang aan de toekomst* (Nijkerk, 1969), p. 57.

the Churches, we may expect a new and more authentic public recognition. This can already be observed in a modest measure among scientists who turn to Scripture to rediscover the ultimate concern of their scientific labor and its results.[50]

Finally this process also has an ecumenical effect, as may be gathered not only from a common translation of the Bible [51] but also from the growing awareness that the authority of the Bible cannot be divisive and schismatic as long as the authority inherent in Scripture itself is not used to set up a separate home outside or inside the house of God. As Scripture delivers us from possessiveness, power and validity issues, it will itself acquire a new importance. The problem of the decreasing importance of Scripture, which we have outlined above, will then prove to be a breach through which we can leap into the future.

[50] Cf. "Prophets in the Secular City," in *Concilium* 37 (1968), pp. 133-50; G. Picht, *Der Gott der Philosophen und die Wissenschaft der Neuzeit* (Stuttgart, 1966), pp. 68-106.

[51] Cf. P. Reymond, "Vers une traduction française oecuménique de la Bible," in *Verbum Caro* 86 (1968), pp. 52-65; "Coopération avec l'alliance biblique universelle," in *Information Service* (March 4, 1968), pp. 6-9; "Guiding Principles for Interconfessional Cooperation in Translating the Bible," in *Information Service* (June 5, 1968), pp. 22-25; "Cooperación con la Iglesia Catolica para la traducción y difusión de la Biblia," in *Criterio* XLII (March 1969), p. 136; E. Maron, "The Search for a Common Bible," in *Scripture Bulletin* 1 (April-June, 1969), pp. 26-37.

## BIOGRAPHICAL NOTES

ROLAND DE VAUX, O.P.: Born in Paris in 1903, he was ordained in 1929. He studied at the Faculty of Literature at the Sorbonne and at the Dominican Faculty of Saulchoir. He gained degrees in literature, Scripture and theology, and is professor of Israeli ancient history and of Palestinian archeology at the Ecole Biblique of Jerusalem, of which he is also a director. He is an editor of the *Bible de Jérusalem*, of *Collection des Etudes Bibliques*, and of *Cahiers de la Revue Biblique*. His publications include the two-volume *Les Institutions de l'Ancien Testament* (Paris, 1961 and 1967), and *Les Sacrifices de l'Ancien Testament* (Paris, 1964).

DENNIS McCARTHY, S.J.: Born in Chicago in 1924, he was ordained in 1956. He studied at St. Louis University, at the Freie University in Berlin, and at the College of Higher Studies in Paris. He also attended the Catholic Institute in Paris and the Pontifical Biblical Institute in Rome. He gained degrees in the arts, Scripture and theology, and is associate professor of biblical languages and literature at St. Louis University. He is also advisory editor of *Theology Digest* and *The Way*. His published works include *Treaty and Covenant: A Study in Form in the Ancient Near Eastern Documents and in the Old Testament* (Rome, 1963).

JOSEF SCHREINER: Born in Germany in 1922, he was ordained in 1949. He studied in Germany at the University of Würzburg, and in Rome at the Pontifical Biblical Institute. He holds degrees in Scripture and Old Testament exegesis, and a doctorate in theology, and since 1964 he has been professor of Old Testament exegesis at the University of Münster. His publications include *Die Zehn Gebote im Leben des Gottesvolkes, Dekalogforschung und Verkundigung* (Munich, 1966), and *Von Gottes Wort gefordert. Aus der Botchaft des Propheten Jeremias* (Düsseldorf, 1967).

CHRYSOSTOME LARCHER, O.P.: Born in France in 1908, he was ordained in 1932. He studied in Lyons, both at the Catholic Faculty and at the Dominican House of Studies, and then in Jerusalem at the Ecole Biblique. He holds degrees in literature, theology and Scripture, and is bursar for the Dominican convents in the provinces of France. Besides contributing to the *Bible de Jérusalem*, he is an editor of the *Bible oecuménique* and the author of *Études sur le Livre de la Sagesse* (Paris, 1969).

JOHN CROSSAN: Born in Ireland in 1934, he studied at St. Patrick's College, Maynooth, and then at the Pontifical Biblical Institute in Rome and at the Ecole Biblique in Jerusalem, receiving a degree in Scripture and a doctorate in theology. He has been professor of biblical theology at the Catholic Theological Union of Chicago since 1968. He is a member of the Chicago Society of Biblical Research, and also of the Catholic Biblical Association and the Society of Biblical Literature. His publications include *Imago Dei. A Study in Philo and St. Paul* (Rome, 1961) and *The Gospel of Eternal Life* (Milwaukee, 1967).

ULRICH LUZ: Born in Switzerland in 1938, he was ordained in the Reformed Church in 1963. He studied theology at Zurich and at Gottingen, receiving his doctorate in theology in 1967. Since 1968 he has been *Private-Dozent* of New Testament studies at the University of Zurich. His published works include *Das Geschichtsverständnis des Paulus* (Munich, 1968).

STANISLAS LYONNET, S.J.: Born in France in 1902, he was ordained in 1934. He studied at the Catholic Faculty of Lyons, the Jesuit Faculty of Lyons-Fourvière, at the Sorbonne School of Higher Studies in Paris, and at the Pontifical Biblical Institute in Rome, receiving a licentiate in literature and a doctorate in biblical studies. Since 1943 he has been professor of biblical theology and of New Testament exegesis at the Pontifical Biblical Institute, where he is also the vice-rector. His published works include *La nature du culte dans le Nouveau Testament. La liturgie après Vatican II* (1967) and *La loi et la liberté du peuple de Dieu* (1968).

JEROME MURPHY-O'CONNOR, O.P.: Born in Ireland in 1935, he was ordained in 1960. He studied at the Dominican House of Studies in Ireland, at the University of Fribourg in Switzerland, at the Ecole Biblique in Jerusalem, and in Germany at the universities of Heidelberg and Tübingen. He is professor of comparative biblical studies at the Ecole Biblique. His publications include various writings on St. Paul and the New Testament, and he contributes regularly to *Revue Biblique*.

THOMAS WORDEN: Born in England in 1920, he was ordained in 1946. He studied at the University of Fribourg in Switzerland, at the Pontifical Biblical Institute in Rome, and at the Ecole Biblique of Jerusalem, gaining degrees in theology and Scripture. Since 1968 he has been a lecturer in biblical theology at Upholland College, England. His published works include *The Psalms Are Christian Prayer* (London, 1962), and *The Sacraments in Scripture* (London, 1966).

FRANS NEIRYNCK: Born in Belgium in 1927, he was ordained in 1953. He studied in Belgium at the Major Seminary of Bruges, and at Louvain University, receiving a licentiate in biblical philology and a doctorate in theology. Since 1968 he has been dean of the Flemish section of the theological faculty of Louvain University. His published works include *La redaction matthéene et la structure du premier. Ephemerides Theologicae Lovanienses* XLIII, pp. 40-73 (1967).

# Subject Index to
# CONCILIUM
# (Volumes 41-50)

International Publishers of CONCILIUM

ENGLISH EDITION
Paulist Press
*Paramus, N.J., U.S.A.*

Burns & Oates Ltd.
25 Ashley Place
London, S.W.1

DUTCH EDITION
*Uitgeverij Paul Brand, N.V.*
*Hilversum, Netherlands*

FRENCH EDITION
Maison Mame
*Tours/Paris, France*

JAPANESE EDITION (PARTIAL)
Nansôsha
*Tokyo, Japan*

GERMAN EDITION
Verlagsanstalt Benziger & Co., A.G.
*Einsiedeln, Switzerland*

Matthias Grunewald-Verlag
*Mainz, W. Germany*

SPANISH EDITION
Ediciones Guadarrama
*Madrid, Spain*

PORTUGUESE EDITION
Livraria Morais Editora, Ltda.
*Lisbon, Portugal*

ITALIAN EDITION
Editrice Queriniana
*Brescia, Italy*

POLISH EDITION (PARTIAL)
Pallottinum
*Poznan-Warsaw, Poland*